Boom!

Boom!

The Life and Times of a Suicide Near Death Experiencer

Chris Batts

Editor: Katie Connolly

Cover Photography: Chris Batts

Cover Design: Anthony Picco

The events and conversations in this book have been set down to the best of the author's ability. Some names and details have been changed to help protect the privacy of individuals.

The cover image is of the actual location of Chris's near death experience.

Dedication

I dedicate this book to Uncle Rabbit. I thank him for being in my life and loving me like his own. So many times when I've gotten stuck in a situation, all I needed was to ask what would Uncle Rabbit do and I had my answer.

Acknowledgments

I have so many people to acknowledge including George Williams, a very intellectual person who reminded me to keep my eye on the prize for positive things and always encouraged me. Another person I want to thank is Katie. She's helped me with this whole book writing process. She has always been there for me and has helped me more than anyone can imagine. Then there is all the support from my incredible friend Sidney. She helped me see that you could still have fun in the littlest things every day. She reminded me that no matter what comes up in life, some people would love to have your problems.

I also want to mention several people who have inspired me in my career. One is a very experienced teacher named Kim. Much respect to her. Kim helped me become a better para educator, as did Miss G. I also want to thank two top para educators. Hayley and Lexie are among the best. When we work together, I just watch and learn. They are amazing at what they do.

Finally, Janet is an incredible person with a heart of gold. She is always willing to help people and expects nothing back. She supported me after my near death experience and just with life in general, showing me how the glass is half full. Since I have been around her, instead of looking at the worst, I've been looking at the best.

Table of Contents

Introduction

The suicide rate is rising[1]. Many people think about suicide every day. A lot of these don't actually attempt suicide, but I did. During my suicide attempt, I crossed over to the other side. I met God and those I call angels in the spiritual realm.

I had what is known as a near death experience or NDE. An NDE is defined by the International Association for Near Death Studies (IANDS) as a "profound psychological event that may occur to a person close to death or who is not near death but in a situation of physical or emotional crisis." NDEs often have common features, but each is different and unique to the individual. Aftereffects of an NDE often include increased intuition and heightened empathy and understanding of others.

This book gives my background on what I knew and felt leading up to the moment where I jumped out of a car and died. For years, I was depressed like many people. I was traumatized by a physically and mentally abusive family who didn't want me. In spite of this, I learned how to stand up for myself. I was able to connect with every kind of person. Even the most hardcore gang members respected my individuality. My friends became my family.

---

[1] Suicide increased 33% from 1999 to 2017 per National Center for Health Statistics Data Brief No. 330, November 2018. This report also states that suicide is the second leading cause of death for ages 10 to 34 in the United States.

Having grown up in the toughest neighborhoods, I saw what people have to do to fit in. I had to put on an angry face by day even though I had the spirit of love on the inside. If I showed that love to certain people, they got scared. They weren't used to it. I saw how some people in this world have absolutely nothing and barely enough money to shop at the local Goodwill store. I knew what it was like to be that guy who had to walk far distances on the streets with no money for food or a nice cold drink. Life seemed tough at times with no way out.

Before my NDE, I didn't do much deep thinking about the meaning of life, but I felt that I was missing something. Even when I was surrounded by people, I felt alone. I wasn't sure what life was all about other than popularity and fun. Once the good times in school were over, I developed addictions and anxiety that led me to suicide.

The knowledge that I gained from my NDE changed everything. It gave me meaning and purpose that I didn't have before. I never expected to experience what I saw and felt on the other side. I never expected the outcome of being able to communicate with my angels on an ongoing basis in my daily life. I learned how God loves us and we are never alone. This freed my spirit.

Like me in the past, a lot of people feel unloved and struggle in various ways to find love. At the heart of it, many people don't know their true selves. My NDE showed me how God really sees us. You may not be the fastest, leanest, prettiest, sexiest person in the world, but remember this: you are loved by many that you don't even know about. After my NDE, I no longer care about the kind of popularity I had before, where life is all about going to the biggest party. Now I only care about helping others and getting my message out to as many people as possible.

Looking back on my life, love had been there in the form of certain people who helped me learn. One of them was Katrina, older and more experienced in life than I was, who taught me I didn't have to be in the "hood" all the time. I could be anyone if I set my mind to it. You'll learn more about Katrina in the following pages. There were also two other women who crossed my path but aren't mentioned in this book. They showed me tough love—how to be strong and hold myself with confidence. They told me, "You've got this." I thank them for that, wherever they are.

With this book, I hope to reach not just one, but many people who are feeling down. Maybe you think that no one understands what you are going through. Let me assure you that I understand everything you're going through. If you get anything out of my experience, I promise you that while times may seem rough right now, you are loved and things will get better. The afterlife is real, and we have many invisible supporters on our side.

Chapter 1

Being from Nowhere Doesn't Count

I grew up as a boy from nowhere. My city was not exactly a happy place. I still think back to the gridded streets with scrubby, dusty lawns; metal fences protecting small houses with peeling paint; and many vehicles with taped up cracks in their bumpers. It hasn't changed much since then. A lot of people in my city have chips on their shoulders. There are a few gated communities here or there, but it's not exactly for the rich. Many people feel unloved and do whatever they can to survive. People do things like sell their plasma or rob and steal to make their next high. There are many gang members too. They travel in packs. Crips wear blue and Bloods wear red. They hang out on street corners.

In my sophomore year of high school, my life could have ended just like many others who were killed through violence in my city. I was wearing a baby blue jumpsuit and walking alone through quiet streets. It was a dry, sunny afternoon with hazy skies.

"Where you from?" a voice called out. I looked to the left. In a city of gangbangers, with everyone seeking their own forms of power, it was just a matter of time before something like this would happen. I had seen their faces the day before, so I knew they had me spotted already. One had a scar at the tip of his chin and a red bandana hanging out of his pocket. I had seen him reaching back to feel it while he walked.

Another had slightly crossed eyes that made it seem as if he could keep you in his view while also tracking someone else.

They were in front of an open garage door, each wearing something featuring red. The dude who had called out came closer.

"I don't gangbang," I said.

Three more people followed slowly out of the garage as if pulled by the leaders with invisible strings. They glared at me.

"I'm from nowhere," I said.

"No. None of that counts. That nowhere shit don't count," the leader pronounced, waving his hands and shaking his head. "You have to be from somewhere." Others stepped out from the garage, so there were in total eight or nine. They surrounded me.

Inside I thought, "Oh shit! I'm going to die. Am I going to go to heaven or am I going to go to hell?"

I took off my jacket, dropped it, and looked at the circle of dudes. "So what y'all want to do?"

One of the guys studied me closer and I met his gaze. I would still swing on one of them to let them know they would have to fight me.

"Oh, you have heart, huh?" he said.

"It's whatever."

"It's whatever, huh?" One of them pulled out a gun, then another quickly followed. "So, what about now?"

I looked into the muzzles and then looked straight ahead. "It's gonna be what it's gonna be."

I meant it. I turned and started walking away very slowly. I felt they were still pulling out more guns on me.

A bullet hit the ground and ricocheted. I breathed in and focused on the corner at the end of the street. Another bullet slammed into the ground and two others flew over my head. If they had wanted to hit me, they would have.

As soon as I hit the corner, I power walked to the place where I lived, through streets with cracked pavement and everything the color of cement. A lone dog barked behind a chain link fence while a car radio pounded some beats.

Aunt Poochie's house was in a gated community. She lived right past the gate. Every house there looked the same, with a white textured exterior, red tile roof, short wide driveway, and a narrow strip of lawn. It was dead silent except for the traffic beyond the brick walls that surrounded the community.

The large front door of the house was inset and shaded from the sun. Inside, Aunt Poochie sat on the couch with her feet up, watching a huge 60-inch screen TV. She was my mom's oldest sister. Aunt Poochie was the fourth family member who had had custody of me since my mom abandoned me years ago. Over the past few months, I was finding out that she, like the rest, didn't really care about me. The images from the screen reflected in her glasses. Her shoes were off, showing her pedicured toenails.

My whole body was shaking and my heart was pounding. Aunt Poochie glanced at me and asked what was wrong. I told her what had happened.

"Oh," she said, peering at me over the top of her reading glasses, "well, what do you want for dinner?"

I told her I wasn't hungry. I was too shaken up to eat. Perhaps later I'd do the usual and go out with friends and find some food. I had spent a lot of time in the streets since moving there. Aunt Poochie never asked about what I was doing or wanted me to come home. And now when my life had nearly been taken, her response was no different. I had hoped for better things from her. I felt so alone.

I went to my room and looked out the window at the back yard penned in by solid slats of tall fencing. Tomorrow, I would tell all my friends at school about the shooting. They

3

would care and would be impressed at how I got away. Back when I was a little kid and rejected by my mom and family, I had considered suicide often. But I had pushed aside those feelings for several years. Guns pointed at me made me realize how instantly my life could be over.

I suddenly remembered a conversation with my mom from years ago. She had taken me to a gang movie and told me she wanted me to be a gangbanger. I told her I didn't want to. She didn't listen. She went on to say she would be proud of me as a Crip. "Never disappoint me and be a Blood," she said, one of my rare memories of her. If I had listened to my mother, I would definitely be dead.

The last time I saw her was a few years back, there at Aunt Poochie's house. It was during one of our rare family gatherings. My mom abruptly showed up and there were arguments in the kitchen. Her mom, my grandma, was always picking on her. When she spilled some wine, her mother and sisters told her she was stupid. When I tried to talk to her, she told me to get the hell away from her. She hadn't wanted me from the start. I never thought I'd ever feel motherly love in my entire life. This feeling had haunted me from early childhood. It didn't go away for good until I met God and my angels during my near death experience several years later.

Chapter 2

Beginnings

Before Aunt Poochie, there were the days with Aunt Laura, another of my mom's sisters. This was my second home after my grandmother became too sick to care for me. The social worker assigned to me, who came around every so often, was named Marcie. She shook hands with my aunt and uncle each time and always gave me a lollipop.

"Are you happy here, Chris?" she would ask, smiling.

"Yeah, I'm happy," I would reply, looking down. Out of the corner of my eye, I saw Aunt Laura and Uncle Robert watching my every move. I was scared to say I wasn't happy, because when the social worker left I knew I would get beaten again. My aunt and uncle never let me be alone with her. That way they could continue to get their money. After Marcie left, Aunt Laura sent me to my room.

Aunt Laura and Uncle Robert didn't want me, but they did like the money they received monthly for housing me. None of the money ever came my way. They never bought me clothes or shoes. In frigid weather, I went to school in shorts and no jacket. My only jeans were old and contained big holes. I got nothing for Christmas.

I wondered if all families were like this. I didn't think so. The other kids at school talked about their parents, but I had nothing to say about mine. My father had been an 18 year old drug dealer turned addict and my mother 22 years old and pursuing a modeling career. Those aspirations ended when she found out she was pregnant. My father was never in the picture because he had been sent to prison for selling drugs. I was born during his first year in prison and he was in and out of prison for many years after that. Because I never met him or heard from him, I knew that he did not search very hard for his son.

In my room, I undressed and looked at my legs. There were welts on my calves from beatings the day before. I'd gotten in trouble because I was caught stealing someone's snack from the cabinet. The teacher let my aunt know what I did, but my aunt would never admit why I did it. I was never allowed to make a lunch to take to school while my cousin Bobby, their kid, was.

These so-called family members begrudged my presence. I was forced to stay in my room at all times except dinner time and if company came, I couldn't even come out for dinner. I would go in the bathroom and drink the sink water because I couldn't go into the living room or kitchen. I was not allowed to have friends at the house. I was not allowed to talk on the phone. I was not allowed to go to the neighborhood park. Sometimes my teachers asked if I was abused. I always had to lie because I was so scared of my aunt and uncle. I thought that if I were to call the cops, they would beat me worse than ever until the cops came. Somehow, I felt they would get away with lying to the cops as well.

Bobby opened the door to my room and went to play games on the computer. He saw me there and didn't even say hello, so I kept quiet. I was not allowed to use this computer even though I slept right next to it. My cousin got anything he wanted—acting lessons, karate lessons, clothes, and new shoes. My aunt and uncle wouldn't buy me any games although their kid got all of the new game systems. Anytime Bobby and I got into a fist fight, I got in trouble but he didn't.

Many times I was forced to do all of Bobby's chores plus mine, and still find time to do homework. I was so lonely in my room that I played with my pens and pencils as if they were action figures.

I sat at a little desk they had set up for me, looking at my math homework. I was afraid to ask for help, because whenever I had needed help with homework back in kindergarten and first grade, any wrong answer meant a belt to my ass, a slap to the back of my head, a back hand to my forehead, or flick to my ear. Back then, I usually cried all the way through homework. By now, I knew not to ask.

A prisoner in this cruel house, I felt like a dog not a boy. I felt I had been born into a viciously cruel world that I was not ready for. There seemed no reason for me to even be alive. The first thing my grandma ever told me about my mom was that she had thrown me in a dumpster when I was six months old. A neighbor heard me crying, looked in the dumpster, and realized who I was. She then called my grandma. Soon after that, a court judge ruled my mom unfit, so my grandma took me. My grandma was an angry woman, angry at the world. She used to tell me how much she hated having my mom and wished she had aborted her, because then none of us would be here.

I stayed with my grandma until I was four years old when she got sick with a nervous breakdown. Some said it was because of my mom. That's when the court turned me over to my mom's sister, Aunt Laura. On the weekends, Aunt Laura and Uncle Robert took me back to my grandma.

In second grade, we had an event called Grandparent's Day at school. A grandma or grandpa would come and bring cupcakes or some other food. We would all eat at the low kid-sized tables. Many kids had grandparents that came. My grandma said, "I'll just do it," and all morning on Grandparent's Day, I kept wondering if she would really show. I was so excited to think she would come for me. I went to the office and my grandma was there. I yelled "Grandma!" in a happy voice and rushed to give her a big hug because all the other kids did the same. When I did, she said, "Get off me! Oh my God. Get off me!"

My grandma came to class and met a couple of my friends. We had lunch but she ended up leaving after 20 minutes, whispering to me, "You know what, Chris? These kids are working on my nerves. I need to get out of here. I can't be around this many kids. I can't stand kids. I hate kids." I wondered why I was the only kid whose relatives couldn't show some love.

My memories of my mom were few and far between. Once, when I was about five years old, my mom visited on a weekend and took me out. We went to the mall on a bus. My mom shopped for herself and didn't get anything for me. When we arrived back near my grandma's place, my mom was in a hurry to get this visit over with. She had a life far from me that I knew nothing about. She pulled me by the arm and rushed me to the front door of the bus. She knocked into me and pushed me down the stairs. I fell on the concrete, cutting my foot. I wasn't wearing any socks. I was about to cry from seeing the blood. I heard her angry voice from behind, "You better not cry or I will beat you right now. I don't care who is watching." I still have the scar on my left ankle, though it has faded some over the years.

During that same visit, my mom decided it was time to cut my nails. She pulled me into the bathroom and got out the clippers. She then cut my nails so short that they started bleeding. I asked why she had thrown me in a dumpster years ago. Her response was, "I didn't want you at the time!" She told me how lucky I was to be here at all because she could've aborted me.

Before long, there was a lot of yelling and screaming. My grandma was after my mom and my mom would have none of it.

"Michelle, Michelle! Come back here! You ain't going nowhere!" I heard my grandma calling her name. My mom left, slamming the door behind her. My nails were still bleeding. I tried to snack on some grapes but each one I pulled off the bunch stung my raw fingertips.

By age 9, I saw my mom once or twice a year. I was never sure what to expect from her. During each visit, she gave me from $20 to $50. If Aunt Laura and Uncle Robert found out about me seeing her, they took the money away. They teased me, calling me "problem child," "fat boy," and other demeaning names. They looked for any reason to beat me with a big security belt, shoe, or anything else that was handy. We went to church every Sunday and a couple times during the week. I started having seizures at the age of 4 and was diagnosed with ADHD and epilepsy. ADHD is sometimes hard to control. Many times I got into trouble just for talking in class at school. At home, I was punished for talking in church or forgetting to vacuum.

Living with Aunt Laura, I felt worthless and wanted to be out of this world completely. I thought about how to die. One day I cut my wrists in secret in the bathroom using a kitchen knife. I watched the blood swirl down the drain. It hurt enough for me to stop cutting and wrap towels around both wrists. I didn't want anyone to know what I had done, so I bandaged the cuts with washcloths for several days and hid them under my clothes until they dried up. My wrists burned when I showered. I didn't want anyone to find out what I did, but this gave me the sense that there was an escape route that I could take at any time.

Eventually, Aunt Laura and Uncle Robert found out I was allowed to talk on the phone and watch TV at my grandma's house, so they didn't take me there as often. I was frequently locked in my room where I read Harry Potter books. I often compared myself to him because I was in Harry's shoes, with an evil aunt, uncle, and cousin.

Whenever the coast was clear, I called my Uncle Rabbit on the fax phone. I used the fax phone because I couldn't use the regular phone. Uncle Rabbit was my only escape, the only family who cared. He wasn't even a blood relative, but married to my grandmother's sister, Aunt Sara.

Chapter 3

Uncle Rabbit

Everything was different on the weekends when I got to see Uncle Rabbit. He was an older man and in his 70s at the time. Uncle Rabbit was a real man, a country man from Mississippi who loved baseball, wore overalls, and chewed tobacco. Guys wanted to hang out with him and he treated women with respect. This man was not even my blood, but he treated me as his own. He allowed me to watch TV at his house and talk on the phone. Not once did he judge me.

Being a kid with ADHD, I sometimes spilled juice or soda on the floor. He told me it wasn't my fault. He said he understood that I didn't have a mother or father to teach me anything. We would battle at math problems and Bible verses. I didn't take to religion much, but he always welcomed my opinion of it, even though he was a solid Christian. He had frequent friendly debates with his friends about their respective religions. Before Uncle Rabbit went to bed every night, he poured a shot of whiskey. He put the bottle away then got on his knees with a shot and prayer.

Around the time I was seven, I asked Uncle Rabbit if I could chew some of his tobacco. He gave me a string and I watched him to see what to do. As he would spit, I would spit; when he would rinse his mouth out, I'd rinse mine. A few months later I asked to taste his beer. He laughed as I spit it out because of the nasty taste. I tried to be like him in every way, even wearing his hats like he did. At times now, I still catch myself tossing my keys on the table like he did. He used to carry a pocket knife with him wherever he went. I still have that knife. One time, when he wasn't watching, I snuck out to the back yard without my coat, even though Uncle Rabbit had told me not to.

"What are you doing out here, Chris? I told you to stay inside! You haven't done right, Chris. You haven't listened."

He grabbed my arm firmly and brought me inside. He sat me on his lap, turned me, and whooped me a few times. I cried a little. After he was done, his eyes were wet with tears too.

"I'm sorry, Chris. I'll never hit you again." He went to the kitchen and made me a ham sandwich.

Everywhere Uncle Rabbit went, I wanted to go, even if I had to just wait on him in the car. I didn't care as long as I was with him. If I couldn't go with him, I would cry and run after his car. He rented a plot of land about 20 minutes from his house where he planted squash and had fruit trees. I would always want to go with him while he watered and planted new seeds. The garden was enclosed and he had the key to unlock the gate to get inside. Sometimes before we entered the gate he would joke about letting me in and say, "I'm going to lock your ass out!" Of course, he always let me in. I felt the garden was his get away from Aunt Sara.

One day when we were inside the garden I was being playful and throwing the keys in the air. I said to him, "I'm going to lock *your* ass out."

"No, I'm going to lock *your* ass out," Uncle Rabbit laughed and took the keys away. He went out the wooden gate, then closed and locked it. I found myself trapped in the garden alone. I was not tall enough to see over the solid fence. I heard him get in the car and start the engine.

I started crying and hollering. "He left me! He left me!" We had been joking before, but the feeling of being abandoned by the person who loved me the most was terrifying.

Uncle Rabbit came back in less than a minute and said, "Get in the car." We went home. Before long, Aunt Sara came in the door. I was instantly filled with dread knowing she would find a way to pick on me.

Uncle Rabbit and I had gone shopping earlier and he hadn't unpacked all the bags yet. Aunt Sara rummaged through the bags and pulled out a candy bar. "What's this? What did you buy this for?"

"It's for Chris."

"Why'd you waste your money? He's a retarded boy! Going to hell just like his mom."

Uncle Rabbit cursed. It wasn't the first time he'd defended me. I wondered how someone like him could be with someone like her.

"Let's go for a walk," he said to me. Just outside the door, he said softly, "I'm thinking of leaving, Chris."

I knew they argued often. He'd said he was leaving before, but he never did.

"Please don't do that," I said. "Please. You're all I have." It was the truth. So many times I begged him not to go. I'd never told him about the beatings and abuse with Aunt Laura, but somehow he knew.

Uncle Rabbit nodded and looked up to the sky. He stayed.

When I hit 6th grade, Uncle Rabbit's only son became sick from liver failure because he drank so much. This was Uncle Rabbit's son with his first wife who had passed away before he married Aunt Sara. After his son died, Uncle Rabbit died, too, on the inside.

I stayed with my grandma on the Saturday when Uncle Rabbit went to his son's funeral. I will never forget the look in his eyes after it was over. Wearing his black suit and black dress hat, he looked at me and I felt the depth of his sadness. He was telling me in his own way that he was giving up. I was young, but I understood and I just nodded my head at him slowly. Aunt Sara had no sorrow on her face.

I knew he was fading after that. He fell into a deep depression. His breathing worsened because he smoked cigarettes. He was soon diagnosed with bone cancer. In his early 80's, he also developed Alzheimer's. He started to forget where he was and even at times would call me by his son's name. He was taken to a nursing home and got even worse.

The last time I saw him was when I'd just turned 14 and was almost in high school. He remembered me and the two of us had an amazing visit. As I was leaving, he grabbed my hand tightly and looked at me for a few seconds. He opened his mouth to say something then stopped. After a pause, he told me I'd grown up and that he liked the peach fuzz on my mustache. We laughed.

"Take care of yourself," he said. I knew he wanted to tell me something more but couldn't.

A couple of weekends later, I was on my way to Aunt Sara's house to go with her to visit him. To my surprise, my grandma was there. Those two didn't get along. For them to be in the same room, I knew something had to be up. My aunt put water on her face at the sink like she always did. She then told me Uncle Rabbit was gone. He died a couple of hours before we were supposed to see him. The nurses said they'd heard him begging God to take him because he was suffering so much.

I went home to my room to pretend I hadn't heard the news. It hadn't sunk in yet. As a kid, he made me promise that I wouldn't cry at his funeral, so I kept that promise, as hard as it was. I did cry every day after that for a while. Uncle Rabbit had meant the world to me and was the only one who showed me the meaning of love. I was devastated with the thought that I would never find another person like him.

A few years later, Uncle Rabbit came to me in a dream. He was in perfect shape like he'd been before he got sick. He was reading the newspaper like he always did, having a bowl of cereal, dressed in overalls. He told me how proud he was of me, but that he had to go. He got his suitcase and told me to take care of myself, just like the last time I saw him. Then he vanished into a cloud.

Chapter 4

Starting High School with Aunt Sara

It was 5 AM on a school day during my freshman year. I had slept in a chair all night, which meant I barely slept at all. The living room was piled with junk. I couldn't take two steps without bumping into something. My current home, such as it was, was in a one bedroom apartment with Aunt Sara. After Uncle Rabbit died, she became a hoarder. Every piece of furniture was old and smelly. Every morning I had to find a way to clean off.

The living room was my room. I pulled out the fresh clothes that I kept in a plastic shopping bag and dressed in the dark. I went in the bathroom with my towels and soap. I never left them in the bathroom because she might do something funny to them. She would always ask where I kept my towels. When I asked why she wanted to know, she got mad. Since the bathroom door was fixed so it wouldn't close to give me privacy, I barricaded it from the inside with a chair.

Aunt Sara kept the shower head blocked, so I didn't even try to use it. I cleaned myself with sink water. It had taken a couple of months to perfect a technique for bathing while standing. Dressed in my clean clothes, I took my shirt off and soaped and rinsed my upper body with a washcloth. Quietly, I dried off and put the shirt back on. I pulled my pants and boxers down and did the same. Next I did my feet, standing on one leg then the other. The final step would be to lather my neck, ears, and face, then rinse and dry off. The goal was to get it all done without her banging on the door. She liked to rush me out because she claimed she had to pee, but it was only to mess with me. For that reason, I never fully undressed in case she pulled that act on me.

I finished getting ready. Aunt Sara was in the kitchen, washing dishes with towels that were always dirty. Whenever I was moving around, she would force herself to get up just to watch and listen to everything I did. She glared at me but said nothing. I left and slammed the door hard, making the bells on her door jingle.

Life with Aunt Sara was a never ending battle. She constantly tried to control and provoke me while I constantly fought her mind games and defended myself. I hated it. For the moment, I had no other choice than to live with her.

What was I doing with Aunt Sara, you might ask? While I was visiting my grandma one day that past summer, she got a call from Aunt Laura and Uncle Robert. They informed my grandma that I would never return to their house. They had found some lyrics that I wrote. I had started writing rap lyrics at 10 years old and by the time I was 14, I had stacks of songs. Feeling rebellious, I'd written one about Aunt Laura and Uncle Robert in which I called them all the worst names and wished them bad luck. My grandma was so angry about my existence that she didn't want me to stay with her, either. I moved in with Aunt Sara. I got none of my belongings back from Aunt Laura.

Aunt Sara lived alone now, but if you counted insects, she had lots of company. The chair I slept in, like everything else throughout her place, was infested with bed bugs. She refused to get the place sprayed. Until I finally got an air mattress, I sat on that chair for many sleepless nights, getting bitten by countless bugs. My arms, neck, and even legs had painful bumps. Sometimes roaches would appear. When the building's roach sprayer was scheduled, I pulled everything out of closets and drawers, but she would cancel the service, saying she couldn't afford it.

My aunt had a friend who lived on the second floor. One day she asked me why my aunt never stayed long to visit with her. My aunt always told her that she was worried about me, but the truth was that she'd rather stay home and mess with me.

She messed with me in the darkest of ways. She hung a mirror in the narrow hallway so she could watch from her bedroom what was going on in the living room where I slept. There were times when I caught her sleeping with her hand on her head, facing towards that mirror. Anytime I came home and she was in bed, she would turn over to face the mirror that hung in the hall so she could see into the kitchen and living room. Many times I wanted to smash that mirror.

She told people she took care of me and cooked for me. That was a lie. She never lifted a finger. I would never tell her good things about me because she downright wished evil on people. In that small space, I overheard all of her phone conversations filled with bitter, angry gossip and cursing. My grandmother told me that decades back, when Aunt Sara liked a guy one of my aunts was dating, she got someone she knew to "fix" the brakes on that aunt's car. This aunt ended up running a red light and crashing into a pole. My grandma also said that Aunt Sara went to a voodoo priest with Uncle Rabbit's clothes and strands of his hair to cast a spell so he'd never leave. To this day, I wonder if that is why he never went through with the divorce, unhappy as he was.

Being around Aunt Sara made me miserable. I was always pissed off at her. I wished that one day she felt as bad as I did. I tried to stay away as much as I could. At school, I found my freedom and a sense of belonging that I never got at home.

Chapter 5

Standing up for Myself

On the way to school one day in freshman year, I was shoved by a big upper class guy. I had seen him eyeing me up all week.

"Hey, bitch!" he said. He pushed me toward the mud next to a fence so that I stumbled and fell. I was wearing white. Now my clothes were smeared with mud.

I had fought so many people in elementary and junior high that I wasn't surprised by this at all. I got up. This guy was huge, but I was too fast for him. My fists connected with his face and he fell hard. I got on top of him and broke his nose.

Before I knew it, a crowd gathered to watch. When a teacher came, we both ran to class, but later that day, some seniors gathered around me in the halls. I had instantly established myself by showing my outlook on dealing with bullies. I had learned over time that kids will be mean, just like my family could be. If I stood strong, maybe the bully would leave me alone. With some bullies though, you can walk away as much as you want but they are going to keep bothering you and it's not going to stop. You have to know how to fight. You have to know how to defend yourself.

People respected this. I became the scrawny goofy guy that so many people loved. In time, upperclassmen taught me many things. School was my escape from home. A new horizon opened up where I had more people with me than against me. My friends were my family. During sophomore year, my home situation seemed to improve as well.

Aunt Poochie had always been nice to me, so I jumped at the chance to move in with her and Uncle Joe, her second husband. Uncle Joe was a generous and loving man, but Aunt Poochie overruled him. Her house in a gated community had two bathrooms and three bedrooms. At first, I had my own room with new clothes, shoes, and a phone line. The house was professionally cleaned every few days. My favorite show at the time was *Lizzie McGuire*, about the adventures of a teenage girl whose best friend is Miranda Sanchez, played by Lalaine Vergara-Paras. Earlier that year, I met Lalaine in person at a concert. I took a picture with her and we even emailed for a while. I felt like I was on top of the world.

Auntie Poochie's name was really Lavinia, after her grandma. She was the oldest of my grandma's five kids, my mom being the youngest. If there was a Christmas or Thanksgiving when the family got together, everyone would meet at Aunt Poochie's house. She had the biggest name brand TVs and appliances. Everything she did was big. She went on cruises every year. She always updated her vehicles, an SUV one year followed by a Nissan then an Altima. Fine china and cushy new furniture adorned the living room. Aunt Poochie was always pleasant and in a good mood.

Aunt Poochie's first husband showed up one day while I was living at the house. His name was George Williams. After we had eaten some food and made some small talk about school, he took me aside on the couch.

"I see something in you. You are special, and I can tell you are one of God's own. Here is my number. I want you to have it in case you ever need me."

George seemed more like family than my blood relatives. At that moment, I wondered why things didn't work out with him and Aunt Poochie.

You learn a lot about people when you live with them. A few months into my stay, I no longer got the money I knew Aunt Poochie was receiving for having me in the house. The TV in my room was taken. When I got shot at coming home from school, her reaction was complete indifference. Her opinion was if she let me stay in her house and got me chili cheese fries from the drive-through after church on Sundays, she was taking fine care of me.

"You've got my money this week, right?" I asked Aunt Poochie one day when we were both in the kitchen. She was unloading the dishwasher.

"You don't need any money this week, Chris," she said, and kept on working.

"I do! I need money for lunch," I said.

"You should have saved some from last month. I'll give you more money when I've got it. Don't have it right now."

"Yes, you do. I know you have it. And I need money for my birthday party coming up."

"You don't need any birthday party. I've given you plenty as it is."

It was then that I realized Aunt Poochie was all about the money. She didn't even want to give me what was mine. I was mad enough at this situation to move back in with Aunt Sara.

"I'm out of here! I'm gonna get my stuff."

"Then go," she shrugged.

I left. I was so popular at school that I needed to make this party happen no matter what. With the help of my closest friends, I had my 16-year-old birthday party at the bowling alley. It was my only real party in my life, before or since. My friends bought me a huge birthday cake. A girl I was dating didn't like a friend who'd showed up at the party, so they began squabbling with each other. We had to cut the party short, but I still had a ball. As a few of my friends and I were leaving the bowling alley, we walked across a deserted lot to the local indoor swap meet. When we got close, a car stopped and girls came out in sweats. One was my future jealous girlfriend, who wasn't my girlfriend yet. A fight broke out between her and one of the girls in our group. We broke it up. I felt very important that my birthday party was the occasion of all this action.

Chapter 6

Popularity

The summer before I started junior year of high school, I put the old goofy me in the trash and went through quite the make-over. I started working out—pushups and sit ups—and I gained a lot of confidence. My hair went from short to curly and I started wearing chains, sunglasses, and even du-rags because that was the style. I talked differently. I became charming and wanted to know everything about women.

I didn't feel depressed or suicidal. There was no time for that. I felt the point of life was to be popular and to be loved by people in school and I had achieved this. As a result, I had no privacy, no alone time, and no thoughts about anything beyond the next exciting event. Someone was always around, calling, or wanting to hang out.

I'd been well known already, but this year, if someone didn't know my first name, they knew me by the mole on my face. I rapped, so I knew the rappers. I hung out with the varsity jocks. I went from the emo kids, to the thugs, to the Asian kids, to the Mexican cholos. A lot of people, especially the girls, appreciated my makeover. I had a weakness for Hispanic girls and the Spanish language. I loved my white friends and my super ghetto black girls with different colored hair. I loved every single race and type you can think of. School felt fantastic, and my social life skyrocketed. Friends that I hung out with got popular because of me. I was still a little goofy, but I didn't take no shit.

For the first time in my life, I loved myself and was not afraid of what people thought. My painful childhood became a distant memory. I admit I became kind of arrogant and selfish. I went to the mall and took pictures, then handed out prints to girls around school. They were all gone by the time 3rd period came. I was the pretty boy who the guys would ask to hook them up with whichever girl they were into. As I walked into a classroom, everyone was saying "Hi!" to me. Because of my humor, I also had great relationships with security at school, so I always got away with a little more than the average person. Many girls asked me to come to their houses when they were going to be alone. At this point, I was still a virgin, though no one ever believed me when I told them. Let's just say I had a way of making people go with my ideas.

Sometimes people will hate you just because they are jealous. My hater happened to be the captain of the baseball, football, basketball, and track teams. He might have seen me as a pretty boy who wore watches and chains, but I was still from the street and always ready for a fight. The local Crips threatened to whoop his ass for me. When I told them not to, they laughed and told me I needed to introduce them to all those girls I knew.

One day, I was going to pick up my phone from the principal's office after school (students had to drop off their phones there each morning) when six dudes came after me.

"Come here, fool!" one of them said. These were a bunch of cholo dudes, bald with tattooed heads. A girl that one of them was friends with had said something about me that had made them mad. I was so headstrong that I walked fast across the grass toward them. I was surrounded. Out of the corner of my eye, I spotted a guy nicknamed PeeWee who I had known since junior high in Sunday school. PeeWee was small and skinny, but he really knew how to fight.

"Coo-Coooo!" PeeWee called out. He had these special calls with specific meanings among his crew. "Is there a problem here? Is there a problem?"

The cholos stopped in their tracks. I didn't know PeeWee was so well known, but apparently he was.

"No, there's not a problem," one of the cholos said. "This is between us."

"No, Chris here is my family. You got a problem with Chris, you got a problem with me," PeeWee declared. "Soowoo!" In no time at all, one of his friends appeared, someone I'd never seen before, a black guy with curly hair who must have been 6'4". With certain gang members, if you know someone they know, they consider you family, too.

The huge newcomer folded his arms across his chest. "They call me Bear. This is my homeboy, Chris, and if you got a problem with Chris, you got a problem with me."

Looking at Bear, the cholos decided that maybe they didn't have a problem with me after all; they walked off one by one.

Peewee looked at me and said, "If you ever need me, you let my ass know. I got you. Anything."

"Do you need us to walk with you to the bus stop?" Bear asked.

"No, I don't need anyone to walk with me."

Bear looked skeptical. "Oh, you're so hard headed. Don't do anything stupid."

I was fine though. I walked to the bus stop with no problem. I understood the dynamics of gangs. Gangs were formed for protection. A lot of people in gangs don't have family. Their gangs become their family, the loved ones you are willing to go to war for because they go to war for you. They give you money if you need it and make sure you have a roof over your head. To me, the realest gang members showed care and loyalty, two things my home life was sorely lacking. The realest gang members had my back even if I didn't join their gang, and they didn't even ask me to join. They understood that I was different and didn't need a group of people to prove myself.

Every day in the school bus, Eric, Mike, Damien and I were the main leaders. Our position was in the back, talking, laughing, and throwing papers at each other. A certain girl had a crush on me and Eric would kid her about it. She would get angry when I laughed at Eric's jokes. We were always courteous to the bus drivers and talked to them when we got off.

In March of my junior year, my friend Damien and I went to Six Flags, the amusement park. We were meeting new people all the time while being what some called "weird and random." Pepsi was my favorite soda, so we improvised a Pepsi commercial. Holding sodas in our hands and smiling, we approached a group of girls.

"What are you drinking?" I asked Damien in a loud theatrical voice.

"Man, this is Coke," he said.

I made a face. "Ewww, get that out of here! I got Pepsi!" I announced, drinking some with a big swoop of my arm.

"Can I have some?" Damien asked.

"No, get your own!" I said in mock anger, holding up the can. The group broke into wild laughter. We hung out until they left the park with their parents.

We were supposed to go home on the last train, but I thought we should stay and see what happened even if that meant we didn't go home at all that night. Damien agreed. Both our phones were dead so we couldn't call anyone to get a ride. At closing time, we had no choice but to leave. We found a bench a couple miles from the park and sat down to rest. It was cold and we were hungry. I was wearing only a T-shirt and jeans.

I had an idea. Damien and I went inside a Red Lobster and asked for chips, dip, and lemons. We spent our last money on that. As we left the restaurant, Damien snatched a tablecloth on the way to the door.

"Don't ask no questions!" he whispered to me. "This is our blanket for the night." I thought to myself that this must be how homeless people felt, staying outside at night in the cold and struggling to find food.

I used my hat for a pillow and covered us both with the tablecloth in a strip of grass a few blocks away. After we'd gotten about an hour or less of sleep, the sprinklers came on. Luckily a guy that worked in a local gas station let us stay there. He gave us hot chocolate to stay warm and told us we could stay there until his shift ended in a few hours. Between us, we came up with enough change to use a payphone. My friend called his mom. She told us that we had suffered enough and that she was on her way. We hung out in the bathroom at the gas station, repeatedly pressing the electric hand dryer to keep warm. I had heard through a friend that his 19-year-old cousin in the vicinity had a problem with me, so I stood in front of the bathroom mirror practicing my swings in case I had to fight him. If he challenged me, I wasn't going to back down.

My friend's mom finally came and we both got taken home. In the car, I knew how much we had really screwed up that day. Fun and popularity only took you so far when you had no money, no food, no clothes, and no transportation. Back at home, I was dead tired and fell asleep immediately on the air mattress in Aunt Sara's living room. In the morning when I woke, I went back to working on my musical ambitions with my recording software.

My troubles with Aunt Sara naturally continued.

Chapter 7

The Missing Money

Back at Aunt Sara's place, in my closet I had kept $100 in a box sealed with tape. I wanted to save it for a special occasion that I felt could be any day now. When I checked my box one day, the money was gone.

"Have you seen any money around here?" I asked.

"I didn't take your fucking money!"

"I didn't ask if you took it, only if you saw it."

"I can tell you how to spot a thief! Maybe you left it in your laundry clothes."

"Funny because the money was in a box deep in my closet sealed with tape, so how could it be in my laundry? You've got it, don't you?"

Aunt Sara dropped what she was putting into the refrigerator. Whenever my aunt did wrong to someone, like stealing from them or lying about them, she would fumble her words and drop things.

"You know what you can do? You can pack your shit and leave. I didn't take your *hundred dollars*."

"Whoever said it was a hundred dollars? I never told you that!"

"It was that girl Tanya who took it. Or her son." Tanya was a girl I was dating at the time. Her son wasn't even two.

"You know what? When you get to church on Sunday, you should pray for yourself!" I said. "Fuck you!"

29

Church for Aunt Sara was no more than a fashion contest for her to be seen in her newest clothes and to gossip about others. I turned on the TV and ignored her. I was furious and considered her such a hypocrite. If I was capable of hating anyone, I would have hated her. She went out of her way to torment me and make my life difficult at every turn.

Out of the corner of my eye I noticed that Aunt Sara was rummaging in a closet and pulling something out. When she turned around, I saw it was a baseball bat.

"I'm calling the cops on you," she said. "You better not leave now. You can't fuck with me." I didn't respond and just continued watching TV. I thought she was pretending to dial the police, but within ten minutes they rang the bell. Aunt Sara opened the door and went into a crying act.

"He hit me with this bat, officer," she yelled.

"She is lying! She's a liar!" I exclaimed. "I didn't do anything!"

Of course, they didn't believe me. "Should we take him in?" an officer asked.

"No, it's alright, it's alright. Just keep a record of this!" she said, pointing to her arm. There was a bruise. She must have caused it herself. As soon as they left, she looked at me and laughed.

"I told you that you can't fuck with me." She continued laughing and went to talk on the phone, one of her favorite pastimes.

By this time, Aunt Sara was drunk 24/7 and high on pills. I tried to avoid staying with her. She refused to help me get a driver's license when I turned 16, saying I was too retarded to drive and would crash her car. A week later she totaled the car herself while driving drunk. Around that time, I was accepted to work at my first job, which would have been at a fast-food restaurant, Carl's Jr. Aunt Sara never told me that they called to assign me my start date. I went in to the store only to find out that they had called several days before, then when I didn't show the position got filled by someone else.

Aunt Sara kept the money that was sent for me every month. She rarely bought food, but would sometimes give me two dollars for the whole school day. I stayed in the streets with thugs and gang members. Sometimes I slept outside because she refused to let me in. A couple times she changed her locks. I tried to keep enough money for a night in a motel so I could get at least one night's sleep.

One day I was so hungry, I vowed that I was absolutely going to eat something after school. After the bell rang and I walked out the gate, I headed to the local grocery store. I filled a basket with food, slid other items into my pockets, and went to the checkout. I talked on my cell phone with Damien the entire time as a distraction. As soon as the items from my basket were scanned at the register, I told the cashier I had changed my mind and wasn't going to buy anything.

I went to the automatic sliding door. It opened wide. Then I heard the voice of the security guard. "Come here. Empty your pockets now."

Damn, I was busted. I told Damien I had to go and would see him later.

The security guard took me to the back of the store. He threatened to take me to Metro Juvenile Hall if I couldn't get anyone to pick me up. The cops arrived but let me go after a long wait when Aunt Sara finally came for me.

"What are you doing?" she said.

"I don't know. I was hungry."

"It's no big deal! You could have asked me. I would have given you money!" she exclaimed, waving her arms.

"That's a lie," I told her. She became belligerent and put her hands on her hips.

"Well, did you call me?"

There was nothing more I could say; she was putting on a good show in front of the police. We went back to her place where she went into her room after a few shots of tequila.

Chapter 8

Potter's Covenant House

Many people ask me if I had a religious background prior to my near death experience. Well, I sat through services at my Aunt Laura's Baptist church for years early on, but in high school, I sometimes went with my friend Eric to his mom's Pentecostal church.

"Do you want to be saved? Yes? No?" Pastor Caldwell shouted, cupping his hands around his ears. "If you say no, think twice because your immortal soul is at stake. Praise the Lord, amen! I am going to read to you from Isaiah 54. *For you will spread out to the right and to the left; your descendants will dispossess nations and settle in their desolate cities.* In fact, God's going to give you another city, but not necessarily right away. That is the city of the saved. You read in the Holy Book how many stiff-necked people resisted the purposes of the Lord. But what does the Lord tell you? Forget NOT the Lord's promise! You shall see great things, said God. I will bring it to pass, when you have sought God and you have put God first. Then I will bless you, I will give you finances, I will give you resources, I will give you those desires of your heart. You will mark this, that your prayers and your repentance have been heard! Let us worship His Holy Name!"

Applause broke out. Eric and I looked at each other and squirmed in our seats. Eric was there because his mom, who loved him very much, had taken him there all his life and still wanted him to go with her. However, Eric was the outlaw of the church. He had questions about what was taught there. They called him a freethinker, a sinner. They considered me one, too.

After church, I asked the pastor questions. Why do you say we can't kill people but you kill animals to eat meat? That's weird, I said. Why does the Bible say "Thou Shalt not Kill" but there is supposed to be an eye for an eye, a tooth for a tooth? How did we really know this was the right church when there were so many? What about Catholics and their churches? What about all the other religions out there? I was open minded and wanted to hear other opinions, but when I asked questions, the pastor and deacons told me that I shouldn't question God.

This church's main focus was on hell. According to them, even if you lived your whole life right only to make one mistake before the end, then you went to hell. To them, God was this angry person who did not want any sin near him. They told me that God didn't even know you until you went in front of the church to be saved. Something didn't sound right about that. Why would going in front of the congregation make any difference when God knew everything about us? There were so many rules and regulations too. This was the type of church where people were not supposed to have TV in their homes. Computers were sinful too. They read Christian magazines and that was it.

In spite of my questions, or maybe because of my questions, the church members liked me. Often they asked me, "If you were to die right now, where do you think you would go?" I replied that I thought I'd make it to heaven. To them this was a cute answer. They did not take me seriously. I told them that I didn't rob, didn't steal, and hadn't killed anyone. Wasn't this good enough? Not according to them. "Aw, Chris! You need to be saved!" they said.

There were very definite rules at this church. They said, reluctantly, that you could pray at home but the preference was that you pray in church beginning two hours before the service started. To be saved, you had to go in front of the church and have the congregation pray for you. The women of the church were supposed to be praying for the women, and the men leaders would pray for the men. The leaders were what they called deacons or disciples. They were supposed to be anointed. To be anointed, you had to be saved for six months. After that, you could join a ministry, such as the sound ministry to perform music.

For Eric and me, an intrigue had developed at the church. Eric's mom was intent on the sermons, but Eric was watching every movement that a certain young woman made. Becca was one of the saved and married to a deacon. Was it just our imagination or did she turn her legs toward us? And she was wearing a very short skirt. I was watching Mary, who was sitting in the choir. She was about 26, also married to a deacon. She had long hair that glinted when she turned. This amazing intrigue, plus the food, kept us coming back to church. Mary looked at Becca. Then they both looked at us with smiles and giggles. We wondered how this situation would play out.

I had noticed little flirty actions from Mary in the past. At first I wondered if they were real. Walking proudly on her high heels, she would come up to me and say, "I wish I could hang out with you and Eric. I wish I was with you guys." At a party at a saved person's house, Mary kept touching my leg with her leg. "Oh, I'm sorry! I didn't mean to do that," she said.

After the preaching, we went to a picnic where there was Bible study. We first needed to help set up dozens of folding chairs and lots of food. I carried cases of soda to one of the tables. Before I knew it, Mary was walking next to me with a pan covered in foil. It was the best chicken. Her mom made it.

"You're so sweet for helping, Chris. Oh my God, you're so adorable," she said. Her husband was setting up some chairs a few feet away and gave me a cold look. After we had the food and drinks in place, she beckoned to me with her manicured finger. I went over to where she had put the chicken. She started pulling back the foil in one corner, ever so slowly rolling it back, and looking at me the whole time. Her lips were glossy and glinted like her hair.

"Do you want some chicken, Chris? You can have it all!" she smiled.

Inside, I thought, "Whoa! Wow! What is going on here?"

Later, after we ate and gathered for the Bible study, Mary sat next to me although there were many open seats available. Becca sat next to Eric. I heard her laughing and talking to him, talking about how she was so happy with her husband. Meanwhile, Mary was making conversation with me.

"Where is your Bible, Chris?" Mary asked.

"I don't know," I replied with a smile. "I can't read."

"Ha-ha, Chris, you can reeeead," she said, laughing.

I admit that Eric and I both had crushes on these young ladies, but he and I were amazed that such behavior came from the saved. Eric didn't take the bait and neither did I. I found out later that Becca ended up sleeping with the pastor. He got kicked out of the church. How could they say they were saved even though they cheated, while I was sinning just with the music I listened to?

I was confused and saddened by the contradictions. I knew, for sure, that when they spoke of saving souls from an angry God, they were not describing God. I knew God was full of Love. I didn't know how I knew; it was just a feeling inside me. If God loved us all so much he would definitely not have a favorite. But at the time, I had no direct personal experience to support my feeling.

Chapter 9

Drop It Like It's Hot

The summer before senior year was more fun and party time. At a house party with Damien, Snoop Dogg's "Drop It Like It's Hot" was playing. It was dark and chaotic. Bodies were dancing to the beats.

> *"I'm a gangsta, but y'all knew that*
> *Da Big Bo$$ Dogg, yeah I had to do that*
> *I keep a blue flag hanging out my backside*
> *But only on the left side, yeah that's the Crip side."*

From another part of the house, a voice yelled out.
"That's the Blood's side!"
"Yeah!"
Then there were gunshots, one after the other. Damien and I scrambled for the door. My popularity had become demanding, and now, dangerous. I was always invited to the biggest, most happening parties each weekend and was the first to ask my friends if they were going too. I didn't think about life after high school at all. All I knew was that I was alive and having fun with my friends. With what little money I had, I went out to eat or rode taxis back from house parties if I couldn't get rides. My friends and I went to foam parties at an adult bar. These were parties just for teens where lights dimmed on and off as foam came out of the dance floor.

The week before senior year, I got my hair braided. This was a new look as opposed to junior year wearing curls. I wanted to be different and match my new school clothes from the local mall. I woke up to my alarm going off the first day of senior year and told myself, "You are the senior now. You're the shit, man!"

On the high school campus, Damien and I, along with Eric and Mike, acted like we owned the school. Everybody noticed us. I felt heads turning, thinking, "There's Chris, there's Damien, there they go!" I wore sunglasses matching my braids and would videotape certain moments around school with my camera.

I loved being able to walk off campus with my Senior ID for lunch at the burger place or taco joint. While Eric, Mike, and Damien would just stay in one spot, I was everywhere, from the emo kids in black who spoke about death all the time, to the Christians, to every girl you could think of. The hardcore leaders of gangs were calling me "Young Chris" or "little homie". I was asked to join them, but when I said no, they were cool with it. I felt famous. Girls were asking me to call them or were saying that they were my girlfriend even though they were just making that up. I never got mad because it made me feel so good. It was so different than what came from Aunt Sara!

I had no concern beyond the moment. When it came to tests, I told my friends, "Oh, I'll study later." Unfortunately, that didn't happen. One day my guidance counselor called me into his office. I was being sent to continuation school because my grades sucked.

Continuation school wasn't as exciting as what I had been used to. We switched classes only three times a day. We went to Physical Education separately. At first, I tried to focus on academics so I cut down on the parties. I thought I could try just hard enough at continuation school to get back to my home school. I regularly stopped outside my home school to visit all my friends at the end of the day.

Another difference in continuation school was that we used the city bus because we had outgrown school buses. There were always a dozen or more people of all ages waiting for the bus. This continuation school also had a lot of gang members and gang affiliation. In early January, I was walking to the city bus stop when I bumped into a Blood.

"Watch out," he said.

"Tell your mama to watch out," I replied.

He looked at me angrily and pushed me. My right fist went to his chin and my left fist went to his cheek. He stumbled and fell. I waited while he got up. He came after me, swung, and missed. I stepped to the side then hit him square in the nose with a right hand that he did not see coming. I heard something in his nose crack. I hoped it wasn't broken.

He had ten or more friends with him, but surprisingly nobody jumped in. When I saw him the next day, he said he wanted a round two. His friends just laughed at him and said, "Aw, you won't do shit. He messed you up."

I was good with them. They told me, "Don't worry about anything."

Around this time, I had trouble with cops. I was slowly heading to continuation school one day with my headphones on. I was in no rush because I just felt like being late. Without seeing my closest friends every day at school, there wasn't as much motivation for me to be in a classroom. The cops stopped me, saying I was loitering when I was simply walking. I learned that's just how cops are. They harass just because they can. It's a power game for them.

The cops first said I was detained. Then they asked if I had crack or other drugs on me and told me that I was being arrested. They took everything out of my backpack and searched it. I had to put all my belongings back in before they put me in their car. I asked for their badge numbers and they said that was resisting arrest. After they checked my ID, they ended up driving me to the continuation school. At the end of the day, I rushed to Aunt Sara's place to delete the message from the answering machine that said I didn't show up for continuation school. Then I went back to my old home school and told everyone what happened. There was a lot of outrage over the harassment. People knew how wrong it was. It wasn't over yet because I got a ticket for $300. I had to see a judge and went to court. It felt so unjust and aggravating. There was no cause for any of this. This incident really discouraged me.

I thought I would be able to go back to my regular school after my first semester at the continuation school, but I learned that my units were not enough. I felt unmotivated to continue with my education at all. No one from my family had ever encouraged me to study or get good grades, so I dropped out with the goal of writing and recording music at home. I returned to the house parties on the weekends and showed up at my school graduation as a spectator, watching Damien and my old crew walk for their diplomas. I stood in the bleachers cheering, but felt like a failure. Even to this day, after my near death experience, I regret dropping out. I wish that I could go back and graduate with my class.

From that point on, I was all about work.

Chapter 10

Mall Life

The summer after what would have been my graduation, Eric and I were walking through the mall when we were approached by a girl who looked familiar. She was in dress clothes, a black skirt and a blouse, with five other girls holding clipboards.

"Do you need a job?" she asked.

"Hell yeah!" I replied.

"What?" Eric pulled on my sleeve. "Forget this!"

I shrugged him off. "Let's see what happens," I told him.

The girl said she was going to talk to her manager. A few minutes later she asked us into an office down the hall. Inside was an overweight blonde woman who introduced herself as Sally. A few people in the back were sitting in folding chairs watching TVs.

"You know these two?" Sally asked the girl.

"Yes, I knew him from school," she said, pointing to me.

Sally nodded and gave us applications. We quickly filled them out.

"Can you start next week?"

"Sure!" Eric and I agreed. I shook Sally's hand and she looked at me warmly.

As we exited the place buoyed by our success, I told Eric, "Seeee, and you didn't wanna go!"

The job involved being out on the mall floor recruiting mall shoppers into doing movie surveys. If people agreed, we brought them into the office and showed them previews for unreleased films. After that, they would be asked a series of questions about their opinion and reactions.

We had a certain quota to fill. At the start of this job, I always got my quota and would even get surveys for co-workers who needed them. But after a year, my ADHD started to interfere. ADHD made it hard for me to focus and I got bored or distracted easily. I started to show up late or cancel my shifts. During the middle of the shift, I would want to go home early. Sally told me she understood why I was late sometimes. Even though she could cuss like a trucker's horn, she had a huge heart. She created fake surveys to fill the gaps so I could be kept on. This couldn't last. One day I got a call while I was at the barber shop. It was Sally, sounding sad. She told me that the corporate office told her to let me go and she was so sorry. I told her I understood.

Over time, I had gotten to know many people in other parts of the mall. I found a replacement job in Guest Services and was chosen over four other people based on my interview. Guest Services was the booth at the entrance of the mall that sold lotto tickets, rented baby strollers to customers, and much more. I worked with a friend I nicknamed Scheme because she always came up with unusual ways to make money. One of her schemes was to go all the way down to the valley, to the supermarkets in rich areas, and steal liquor bottles by hiding them in her backpack or sleeves. She knew where to hide from the security cameras in each store. She would then go to three or four different cities and sell them at a discount, making pure profit. Scheme was a busy college student who juggled classes, the job at Guest Services, and her other activities. I was renting a converted garage at the time and wasn't earning much at work. Scheme offered to take me with her and show me how to make some extra money. For a few Saturdays, we went to the supermarkets she had cased out. Wearing a long shirt that covered my waist, I tucked liquor bottles in my pants pockets. I easily sold the liquor to my friends or Aunt Sara and her friends. Aunt Sara didn't ask any questions about where I got the bottles. Very soon though, I chickened out from the shoplifting business.

When I was working with Scheme one day, Maria came up to Guest Services. I had known her since the 9th grade. I was so happy to see her that I gave her a big hug.

"Hey Chris, how have you been?" she said, pulling her hair behind her ear with her finger. We had been good friends all through high school but never were a couple because either she had a boyfriend or I had a girlfriend. There was something special between us, though. There were times, as some parties died down, when we were up all night until the sun came up talking about anything and everything. We would walk to school in the mornings together. Secretly, I had a huge crush on her.

As I looked at Maria's face, those old feelings came rushing back even stronger. There was no one else for me. I had complete focus on her. We exchanged numbers, and we had a phone conversation that lasted all night.

"You know what? I like you," she said at the end.

"And you know what? I like you too," I replied.

"So does that mean I'm your lady and you're my man?"

"Well, of course it does. I've been wanting you since 9th grade!"

"Oh my God, so have I!"

It felt like magic. I was in a new phase of my life. There was nothing standing between us now. I had a place, a car, and a job. And all the while, I was making time to do what I loved: recording music. So far, I had recorded five albums and one mix tape. I didn't write one lyric down. They were all off the top of my head. My delivery was good and writing down lyrics seemed like cheating. I outshined anyone I worked with without even trying. I wanted to be the next Jay Z and I was on my way to being noticed. I would keep working hard, and Maria and I could be together forever.

Chapter 11

Happiness

A year later, I found myself in the landscaping business with Maria's father, Eddie. He owned his own company and was his own boss. Eddie's face was sunburnt and lined from years of working in the sun. He wore wet rags on his head in the hot weather. He barely smiled, but whenever his ranchera music was playing, which was often, he whistled along. We rode in his truck across the highways and suburban streets with a full schedule of jobs from Monday to Friday. We would work for hours mowing lawns, chopping trees, trimming bushes, and giving estimates on work for people's homes. Each morning we saw the rising sun together. We would typically start around 7 AM and end in the middle of the afternoon.

If Eddie's back ever hurt from bending and lifting machinery, he never let me know. One time I saw his hand bleeding from a deep cut. He bandaged it himself with a kit from his glove compartment and kept on working. Whenever I wasn't doing something right, he would show me how to do it "con muchos huevos!" which meant "with much balls!" As he demonstrated the stronger, more effective way, he would hit the dirt a little harder with whatever tool he was holding. He liked to walk around with no shirt. Even though he was really buff, you could see his gut. For lunch, we would stop at a place where he had called ahead to have sandwiches pre-made. I came to love his favorite Mexican fruit drinks.

Maria's house had a special mystique for me. It was striped white and blue with a large front porch. For the longest time, I hadn't been allowed in. Just like in high school, whenever we saw each other, we would be meeting outside. We spent many hours on the porch. On Halloween, I presented her with a dozen roses for no reason. Maria's mom giggled and told her I was a keeper. Her little brother Jorge would join us out there. In the beginning he would come along on our dates to make sure nothing funny was happening.

After working with Maria's father for several months, Maria's mother, who was a stay-at-home mom, invited me inside. It was an evening when Eddie had to pick up supplies, so he had driven off.

"Do you want some fruit?" she asked me from the doorway.

"No, it's OK," I replied with a smile.

"Why don't you come on in for a while? It looks cold out there," she insisted.

After the momentous occasion of stepping inside, Jorge pulled me by the hand. He showed me all around the house, from Maria's bedroom on the left to her parents' bedroom and bathroom on the right. Maria's mom had an altar covered with pictures of angels and dead loved ones. After I had stayed a while and was looking to walk home, Maria's mom pulled me to the side and said, "Shhh, don't tell my husband but I'm giving you a ride home."

I was slowly becoming part of the family. Maria's mom barely knew English so she would speak English to me and I would speak Spanish to her. I started calling her "madre". She believed in the power of cooking and cleaning. She would always tell Maria that she should cook for her man and make sure he ate. I started being invited to dinner on a regular basis. Jorge begged his parents to let me stay in the house overnight. I did this often, especially after a long day at work. Finally, one day when we came to the door of a new client, Eddie introduced me as his son.

We took a group trip to Disneyland. Maria's parents paid for me. My favorite character then as now was Goofy. I found Goofy and took so many pictures. We went on all the rides. Eddie showed no emotion as one of the rides started, going up...up...up...slow...slow...slow. As the roller coaster whooshed down, he held onto his hat and screamed like a girl. I'd never seen him like that. That year, we had Christmas together, sitting down for a huge dinner with a prayer of thanks for everything we had.

Sometimes Maria would come to my place to watch TV and play games, from video games to card games to board games. Eventually Maria decided to move in with me in spite of her parents' disapproval. My landlord and I went to her house to pick her up and move her stuff. Every Friday we watched a Nick Cannon movie called "Love Don't Cost a Thing" and ate chili cheese fries. We had them again in celebration when President Obama won, the first President we had voted for.

For Valentine's Day, while Maria was at work, I went to the store and bought her a silver necklace and boxed it. I took index cards and left clues starting at the door. The first read, "Remember when we went to Disneyland? I love you, now look under the couch." Maria couldn't stop smiling as she pulled up the huge couch pillow to find a card that read, "I love you and want you to know how beautiful you are. Now look by the computer chair." Next to my silver laptop, the clue read, "I forgot to tell you I love you. You're getting closer, now go to the bed." Maria found red roses there with a final clue to look under the pillow. She was blushing as she opened the package.

"Oh babe, it's so wonderful! It's so beautiful!" Maria gushed. Together we worked on putting the bracelet on her wrist, which is always a struggle with its tricky clasp. We looked each other in the eyes and hugged.

Chapter 12

Breakup

It all began when Maria's mom met Aunt Sara at Maria's birthday party. They did not like each other. My aunt was drunk as always. She and Maria's mom argued and almost ended up fighting. Aunt Sara started telling them that I was a liar and that she had cooked for me back in the day.

Maria's mom started to feel differently about me. Both older women started poisoning things for Maria and me. I stopped trusting Maria's parents. They used to like me, and still acted happy when I gave Maria money or flowers, but now they were saying bad things against me even though I had a job, a place, and a car. Maria's mom told her that I didn't love her. I started feeling like I wasn't listened to anymore. Maria listened to her mom and let her parents control our relationship. It felt like it was always me against all of them.

Meanwhile, Aunt Sara told me that Maria cheated on me with many men including her own dad (I later understood this kind of thinking came from stuff Aunt Sara had done with her cousins when she was younger). I didn't believe this, but the negativity in all directions made me feel alone. Even when Maria and I were home, we didn't talk much.

Around this time, I found out that Maria was sending letters to her ex-boyfriend in jail. I found an unsent letter in a drawer telling him that she missed him and that he would never be replaced. I asked her about it. She said she was just keeping in touch with him while he was lonely and it wasn't a big deal. She didn't know I saw her kissing the letters when she thought I wasn't looking. I figured I could do whatever I wanted too. One day, Maria found a text message on my phone from another girl. Her name was Cassie.

During the months when our relationship was deteriorating, I had gotten back in touch with a girl I knew in 11th grade. Cassie came briefly to a clothing store where I was working and gave me her number. At first, we texted. Next, we spoke on the phone when Maria was out. I started doing things with Cassie in secret. Cassie was wild and free and fun. She was a party girl while Maria liked to stay inside or go bowling. Cassie made it seem like my opinion mattered. This drew me closer to her at the time. She was rebellious with her mom and would find ways to do what she wanted and see me any way she could. After we hung out, Cassie dropped me off a block from our place so Maria thought I walked home.

Now that I look back, I see how immature I was, but at the time, I was drawn to the person who made me feel good rather than the situation that was bringing me down. After finding out about Cassie, Maria said she didn't want to break up and neither did I, but soon after, we found ourselves arguing about everything, even the stupidest things. Months passed and our relationship went further downhill. Then on a Wednesday morning before she was going to work, Maria took a pregnancy test and it was positive. I went along to her first few doctor's appointments where we found out it was a boy. I would always try to cook for her and the little baby we called the "little peanut." She always told me that no matter what, I would be part of my son's life. Then she found out I had cheated with Cassie after one of our big arguments many months earlier. She told me she was disgusted and she didn't know if she could ever forgive me.

Maria and I broke up when she was six months pregnant. She moved back in with her mom and dad. She would write to me now and then when she felt like it. It was a week after it had already happened that I found out that my son was born. Maria completely changed her mind on letting me see him. I saw him briefly when he was a month old and then when he was two. After a couple years of begging to see him and being denied, I went to the courthouse and filed for visitation. We did a DNA test and my visitation rights were granted.

Chapter 13

Anxiety and Addiction

After the breakup with Maria, I started experimenting with drugs. Because I used to have epilepsy as a kid, I went to the doctor and told him I was having seizures. That way I could get prescription drugs and try to overdose on them. I ended up experimenting with those pills, taking them every few hours.

Something else started happening too. Maybe it was my abuse from childhood coming back. Whenever I would go to certain places and see crowds of people there, I would get nervous and start freezing up. My body would shake and my stomach would hurt. I felt scared and paranoid, thinking that everyone was against me. This feeling hit me even when I was playing basketball. I started thinking people were criticizing my every move. I felt angry because I didn't want to feel that way. It began to depress me to the point of suicide, although I didn't do anything suicidal yet.

I didn't go to any doctor for my social anxiety. I wasn't even sure what to call these feelings or thoughts at the time. I found how easy it was to self-medicate with prescription drugs. I was introduced to drinking too. One time someone in my neighborhood was killed in a fight over a girl. I went to my friend Aldo's house to hang out; this was the way we mourned these events in our neighborhood. Aldo's dad was there. I saw some Mexican liquor in the living room.

"Hey Feo," Aldo's dad said, having given me the Spanish nickname Ugly. "Do you want a drink?"

"No thanks, *'Orrible'*," I said, countering him with my Spanish nickname for him, Horrible.

"Well, I know you don't drink. But if you want to you can!" I noticed there was Bacardi in addition to the Mexican liquor. Impulsively, I opened the bottles and took waterfall swigs of each. I thought this was what you do when you drank.

"Dude," Aldo said in disbelief. "You aren't supposed to mix your liquor." I wasn't aware of any such rule. But I felt good and happy in a sudden rush, like I was floating on clouds.

"Jesus is going to be mad at me because I'm drunk!" I announced with laughter, thinking back to the Potter's Covenant Church. Soon Aldo was laughing too.

"Dude, you're not going to get drunk just from two sips," he said. I had a little more. I felt so free and confident. But later I ended up with the worst hangover ever and vowed not to drink for a while.

Meanwhile, my social anxiety grew to the extreme. I got social anxiety just driving my car. My mind kept racing into obsessive thoughts. What if someone saw me and made fun of how I was holding the wheel? How my face or hair looked? The way I sat—was it too high or too low? Was my outfit alright or was my car too old? When I went on a bus, more paranoid thoughts came up. Were people I knew going to be there? It started getting worse and I avoided the bus. As I walked, I became scared I would see someone I knew pass me in their car. I didn't even want to talk on the phone because I thought people would judge me for the way I spoke or sounded. I was worried about everything. If I was walking, I wondered if someone was going to make fun of how I walked. At home, I would constantly look in the mirror. Did my shirt and pants fit? Were they too small? Too big? Did they match? When I was around new people who weren't looking at me but were talking to each other, I started thinking they were talking about me and making fun of me. When anxiety spells hit, I would go on auto pilot. From the outside, I might be doing amazing, but on the inside, I was beyond miserable. Social anxiety made me want to hide from the world to be more comfortable. I was trying to go back to school but anxiety overwhelmed me there as well. I took a Deaf Studies class and procrastinated giving my mandatory presentation until the last slot on the last day. In a strange daze, I went through my presentation. Everyone told me I killed it and looked so comfortable, but the whole time I tried to avoid eye contact and stare at the ceiling. I didn't even want to see a person's head. If I had looked at one person in the eye, I would have forgotten everything. I took an English course too. I was doing great for the whole semester but in order to pass, everyone had to make an oral presentation in front of the class. I was so nervous that I didn't show up for the presentation. I failed the course.

With a problem like this, you can imagine the effect on my work. I had a brief stint at a clothing store. My anxiety got so bad I didn't want to work at the register because I thought people would make fun of me for not counting the money fast enough. I constantly thought about how I would screw up. When inventory was delivered, boxes would be thrown at you from the trucks. I was terrified they would throw a box at me that I couldn't catch and I would be mocked for dropping it. Before that hypothetical situation happened, I stopped going to work at all. I became unemployed. When I went to the local county building to get assistance, I felt everyone was looking at me and laughing at me for some unknown reason.

It spiraled out of control. My confidence sank to near zero. I didn't believe in myself and felt like my life was not worth living. I found support in kind and loving people who saw the good in me. I was crossing the street one day with groceries when I saw a new crossing guard, a beautiful Hispanic girl with long black hair and glasses. She held up her sign for me when I was crossing the street. She smiled at me and seemed very sweet. After several more meetings, I offered her my number.

"I think you're pretty and you seem really cool. I want to ask you for your number but I'm not going to. I'm going to give you mine." This was my way to see if she would actually respond.

"Oh, okay! I would love to text you later!"

Angie did. She told me about herself in much more detail. I found out that she was a motivated person who loved surfing. She was always going to the gym and running. In time we started hanging out. She opened up to me that she had struggled with her weight in the past. I started opening up to her about my depression and she always comforted me. One day depression hit me especially hard as I visited her while she was wrapping up her day. It was the first time I had told anyone about the depth of my dark feelings. As we spoke, I fingered a bottle in my pocket.

"Angie, I'm feeling very suicidal."

"Aww, my Christopher, don't feel bad about yourself. You are someone special," Angie said. "Don't do anything stupid."

"I'm not so sure, Angie. You don't know all I've been through." I told her a little bit about my parents, how I didn't know who my father was or where my mother was. I told her how I had seen my mom only once since high school when I was back at the clothing store. I figured my grandma had told her I was there. The only words my mom spoke were,

"Wass up, Chris?" and even that without much heart. My mom averted her glance and didn't want to look at me. She gave me a one-armed hug and went out the door, just like she always had.

I told Angie about Maria, how I cried for days and threatened to kill myself after we broke up. I told her about my son and my struggles to see him. At that point, I hadn't been working for a while either. I felt I didn't have much of a future. Angie started to cry a little and gave me a hug.

"Promise me you won't do anything to hurt yourself, Chris," she said. Angie had to go to her second job. I nodded. "I have to go, but I'll see you tomorrow. I'll see you!" she said.

"I'll see you!" I replied with what energy I could muster.

After she drove away in her truck, I popped five pills at once. As I was walking to my place, I blacked out. When I came to, I was bleeding because I had fallen down on my nose. That day I gave up on pills. I didn't see Angie for a while after that because her schedule changed. When I ran into her briefly the following year, she was doing well and pursuing a career in the medical field. I felt so far removed from a happy, successful life like that.

Quickly, I found a new addiction. It was promethazine mixed with cough syrup, Sprite, and dissolved Jolly Rancher candies. I would stir it up and drink it quickly. I told Aunt Sara I had a cold so she got the cough syrup for me and I bought it from her. A lot of people down South call this concoction "Purple Lean" because it makes you lean to the side when you walk. In your mind, everything becomes slow.

I hadn't been planning on celebrating my 21st birthday but my friend Mike insisted. He told me over the phone, "I don't care what you say. We're going to celebrate your birthday."

Mike came over and picked me up. We went to my old friend Eric's apartment where I was offered weed for the first time and took two hits. I started coughing. My lungs burned like they were on fire. It really hurt. I couldn't believe people would do this to themselves, but I was told that I would get used to it. I also had some rum. I found how easily it eased my anxiety. I started getting into drinking heavily after that. Eventually I had many bottles in my room. I wasn't much of a beer fan but I owned any hard liquor you could think of. I took about five shots before I left the house every day. This went on for several years.

I ended up working for a record label as a producer. I pressed play and stop and mixed tracks while another person recorded. At the studio, some people drank while others would smoked or popped pills. The main owner, when he came in, would chew a mysterious stick that got him high. That's how people got creative in the studio. Substances expanded their minds to develop lyrics for a song, a certain melody, a sharp punchline, or an amazing metaphor. While high, it was easier to let loose, forget about everything, and be fearless. When we heard the best material, we would say, "Dang, they must have been drunk," or "Man, they were high when they came up with this!"

On occasion, I met up with the record label owner at one of the local malls. I visited his large house and saw his Jaguar. They heard me rap at the label and encouraged me to record. I wrote songs for people to sing, but I felt overwhelming anxiety when I had to work with new people. I couldn't think of what to say. I felt more free and confident if I had been drinking, but many people said they heard me slurring my words. I knew I had a problem. Underneath I was still depressed, but I didn't think about suicide much because I was drunk all the time.

I ended up overdoing it one night. Not even realizing what I was doing, I drank a whole bottle of cheap vodka with not one ounce of chase. I had my headphones on with music playing. I was listening to depressing music to match my mood. With the whole bottle gone, I felt amazing. I called all my loved ones and told them I loved them. The next day I woke throwing up. It didn't stop for one week straight. I had alcohol poisoning. I never got that drunk again. I cut back on my drinking and worked more hours at my job. I put a lot of my anger and suicidal energy into my songs. It was around this time I met Katrina.

Chapter 14

Anything Goes

This woman stood out to me. I saw the bright red of her lipstick as she waited in a corner of the club. A number of girls were dancing right by her but she wasn't moving, just staring ahead and looking cool. I went up to her.

"What are they doing?" I asked her over the loud music.

"I don't know," she shrugged her shoulders. "Anything goes." We danced a couple of songs. She seemed to know a few other people there and nodded to them across the room. She told me her name was Katrina.

"What are you doing after?" she asked. I gestured to my friends. "Oh. Why don't you come hang out with me?" she offered. Of course I accepted. She said goodbye to her friends and I said goodbye to mine, telling them not to worry about me because I had a ride home already. I ended up going to her apartment.

The next day she made eggs. Everything in her house was so elegant, from her car to her outfit to even the trash can in her room. I wasn't used to people like that or living like that. To me, it looked like someone famous must be living there. Most of the people I knew had nothing.

Katrina and I hung out more and more. She was older than me and so were her friends. I met all her friends from her job. Her friends made me want to be at their level, with cars, houses, and great careers. Katrina introduced me to the idea of making my life better than what it was. Until then, I had thought of myself as a typical hood guy in the street all the time, a person who had no worth. I learned it didn't have to be that way. I could learn how to change my situation.

Katrina knew all about specialty foods. We took trips to Los Angeles to a restaurant that had certain pupusas that she loved. She loved Williams Sonoma high-end home furnishings and cookware at the mall too. She was cooking all the time and made sure I never went hungry. Whenever I needed something to eat or some small favor, she would help. I ended up gaining weight for the first time in my life. I thought we were in a relationship of some kind. Over time, though, we turned out to be in completely different places in our hearts and minds.

"It's so nice here," I said to her as we rode back from a day trip to Los Angeles.

"It's been another fucked up day," she said. Katrina's phone buzzed. At the stoplight, she pulled gold dangle earrings out of her purse and adjusted them in the review mirror of her car.

"I thought you hated wearing earrings," I remarked.

"I'm going to a girl's night. I'll drop you at your place on the way," she replied. Her phone buzzed again and she picked it up. She seemed slightly amused by the text and quickly replied. I waited a minute, until she put the phone down, watching the expression on her face.

"Is that about the girl's night?"

"Yeah," she answered with a faint smile. The radio station started playing Flo Rida and Katrina's face showed approval. She pointed to the car radio. "He's hot."

I had heard her start many conversations with that phrase. She said it right in front of me to people we met here and there, including her co-workers.

I had noticed a pattern over time. Katrina absolutely loved videos or movies with male rappers or artists. When she heard a song by a new male singer, she'd say, "Oh, I got to see how he looks." She changed the station if a female came on. Every female artist she said was either ugly or had no skill. After spending so much time with Katrina, her opinions started taking over my mind. My perceptions were messed up to the point that whenever I saw T.I., Drake, or Meek Mill, I'd immediately imagine Katrina in bed with them.

At first, I believed Katrina when she vanished for a while or constantly texted others while we were together, telling me it was her girlfriends, her mom, her sister, or her kids. There were days on end when she didn't answer the phone, only to call at random and ask me to hang out. Eventually I doubted more and more if she was being honest. I heard rumors from people and brought them up to her. Katrina snapped back, "Why are you still with me then?"

It was a good question. I couldn't answer it, and the situation began to drain me emotionally. Whenever I told Katrina I loved her, she would respond coldly, "I don't give a shit about you."

At first, I tried to keep my chronic depression and the reasons for it from her, but when we had arguments, which we often did, my depression came back strong. In my own mind, I was not doing well. For the first time in my life, I started doubting the existence of God. I had dealt with so much in my life that it seemed God must not exist if all this suffering and confusion took place in the world. As a result, it wouldn't matter at all if I ended this life.

One time at her place Katrina went outside to get something from her car and I picked up her phone. I was sickened by what I found. It confirmed in no uncertain terms that she had taken action on all those hot dudes.

There were messages from my friends, her sister's friends, her sister's ex-boyfriends, and so many others I didn't know. She apparently was meeting random dudes online. Her phone contained texts stating, "We were supposed to hang out. Where are you?" There were messages along the lines of "I'm home alone" or "I'm kidless" or "I'm downstairs can you help me up?" And there were so many raw pics of her boobs and other body parts exchanged between her and many dudes.

While Katrina taught me about life outside the hood, she also showed me how complicated people can be. My mind was split between the Katrina who lived a great life, who showed me how to rise above the hood, and this other Katrina who acted like a player. Every time I brought up the issue, she point blank asked why I was still with her. In retrospect, I learned that people can be addictions too. It can take months or years to realize this because people are not as obvious an addiction as rum is. I had been pursuing the Katrina-of-the-great-life while ignoring the overwhelming evidence that this was becoming not so good for me. It kept getting worse.

One afternoon at her place, I found more messages on my phone, and could not believe my eyes. It was disgusting to me now. We argued. It ended with her telling me, as usual, that she didn't "give a fuck" about what I thought or did.

Feeling I wasn't important to her or anyone, I left her place, telling her my goal was to get to the train tracks and lie there until the next train came.

I walked to the railroad tracks a few blocks away. I noticed her car, a new Volkswagen, coming up from behind me.

"Come on, get in," Katrina said. I did, feeling numb. Then my phone rang. I didn't recognize the number. When I picked up, it was my mom. It had been years since we'd had contact. I thought she was calling to check in on me, but no.

"Your grandma gave me your number," she said. "But I want you to know that you're not my son. I don't know you. I'm never going to be there for you," she ranted angrily. I couldn't believe what I was hearing. It was an echo of everything I had experienced in my life so far.

"Fuck you. You never were," I told her and ended the call. This confirmed the suicide plan that I'd had in the back of my mind ever since I cut myself secretly in the bathroom as a kid. Here was the cue to go ahead with it right then and now. I didn't even look at Katrina and threw the phone out the window.

"Fuck this," I muttered. I opened the door and jumped out of the moving car. I heard the sound of concrete hitting the back of my head.

Chapter 15

Boom! God

Instantly, I was out of my body though I didn't realize it right away. Somewhere, I heard a voice say, firmly, "I wouldn't do that if I were you." Out of habit, I stood up right where I was. This was in front of a police station and a church. I started to walk to Aunt Sara's place which was close by. I took three steps and the next thing I knew I was in a big white void.

I felt this strong presence. I just knew it was God. God's presence was familiar, strong, and definite. Some things are just so hard to put into words, but when you feel God, you know God in every aspect of your being. Some might call God "Source" but to keep this simple, I will just say God. When I refer to God as male, that's a simplification too. I felt the most motherly love from God who was still the most macho man ever. Instantly, my recent doubts about the existence of God were wiped away.

Next, God basically introduced himself. I didn't see a body or face, but I felt his presence and heard his voice speak telepathically and it was very strong. The first thing I remember and will never forget is hearing these words:

"Yes, I am God, Yes, I am Real. Yes, Angels are Real. They are a gift from Me. Want to meet them?"

I said NO! not with my voice but with my soul. I wasn't ready. I didn't even believe angels existed so how could I handle meeting them?

My thoughts were along the lines of "GET ME OUT OF HERE!" even though there was no physical reason to be scared. In this void, which seemed someplace like the sky, everything was perfect. In that place, your vision is perfect, your hearing is perfect, and everything is perfect. You're not hungry, not thirsty. You're just in your spirit. Nevertheless, I was in disbelief. I didn't think to look at myself because I was scared and uncertain. I thought, "Whoa, this is crazy! This is insane! Humans can't come up with this stuff." Then I thought, "Wait, this stuff really does happen." I was certain that God knew all my thoughts. He knew I was trying to understand what was happening. I had so many questions too. What was God all about? Who is worthy of God's love? He answered my unspoken questions right away because God knows you completely, down to every last particle of your soul.

God started showing me videos. I call them videos but another way to describe them would be visions or demonstrations. First, there was a video of a girl walking. As I saw this, God said, "I love her." After that, there was a video of a skateboarder, just one of those skater dudes who smokes pot all the time, walking with a blunt in his hand. God said, "I love him."

The next video showed a guy walking with a kid, then suddenly the guy reached out and grabbed the kid by his neck. God told me in a calm voice, "I don't like that." He didn't judge them or say anything more than that simple phrase. It was spoken in the calmest voice.

I had more questions. I knew God could hear everything I thought. What about the evil ones or the devil? God just stopped me and I felt him point to the left. I looked way out there to the left and saw a video of this devilish creature wrapped up in chains with a snake wrapped around the chains. I knew it was a symbol just like the videos had been.

That symbol was to tell me not to worry about anything. Evil beings can't hurt me and never will hurt me.

After God showed me that, I had another question.

"God, if I go back to Earth, how do I explain you? When people ask me how you are, how can I explain?" The next thing you know, God gave me the biggest hug ever. I felt him get down to his knees like you do a child, a kindergartener, to speak on their level. I never saw a face but I felt arms around me, filled with love. God just hugged me really tight and I felt so safe. This was how God showed me to explain him to people.

After God let go, all I could say was, "Wow." I asked, "Is there anything you want me to tell these people when I go back to Earth?"

"Go and tell everyone that I love them."

"That's it?"

"That's it." And I thought it was amazing that God loves us so much that he wants everyone to know it. Then God told me another thing. "I will go to the end of the world so that everyone is with me."

I will never forget that message and that feeling. I still get goosebumps thinking about it. I want everybody to feel the same love that God showed me.

Then I saw a bunch of words in capital letters.

"LOVING!"

"CARING!"

"LONG SUFFERING!!!"

I knew what God was saying through those words. He meant them in the same way he described going to the end of the world. He was saying that he is not going to give up on any of you guys.

I asked God how he felt about Earth. God was really sad that people think he doesn't love them. Then...Boom! I met my angels.

Chapter 16

Boom! Angels

Two beings were escorting me, one to my right and one to my left. Their arms were wrapped around mine. I instantly knew these to be guardian angels or guides. There were other beings present but I most strongly recognized the ones beside me. This came as a shock. I did not know this was possible, but there it was, just happening.

The angel on my left side did not look human. He had male energy and was closest in appearance to a large beetle with huge lavender-grey wings. The wings looked thin and had the texture of silk. They were skinny and extended way out. The angel on my right side looked human. He was really buff, really tall, and really huge. He wore blue jeans and a red plaid flannel shirt with his sleeves rolled up to his elbows. He had brown curly hair, tan skin, and was nearly 9 feet tall. His wings were bluish lavender and were tall and wide, extending about 5 to 6 feet. If I was to describe his ethnicity, it would be mixed race, perhaps white and black or Hispanic and black. These two were so strong, so powerful, and so full of light that I felt the impact of their energy would destroy a city if they set one foot on Earth.

"Get me out of here! Get me out of here!" I kept thinking. Speaking and thinking are basically the same there, so the angels both looked at me and told me not to worry.

"Everything is going to be OK. It's OK. It's OK." They kept reassuring me with their kind energy, understanding that it wasn't an easy adjustment for me to take in what I was seeing.

I was so confused. None of this was what I was expecting or had the slightest idea about. I thought after death I might be going to hell because of what I had been taught in church. Not to mention that I didn't even believe in guardian angels in the first place. They weren't part of anything I had ever been taught. Nevertheless, I found myself knowing and understanding so much in this strange place. Recognition and understanding were instant. I looked at the white clouds around me, and I knew that if I went into one of those clouds, I would not be going back to earth.

The angel on my left was stern. I felt him turn to me. I was afraid to look at him. He asked in deep, firm tones, "Are you sure you want to go?" I could feel that he was very strict, but at the same time I knew he hated to see me hurting or overwhelmed. The angel on my right had a ton of patience and understanding. I felt his compassion. He was huge enough to overpower me yet had so much love for me.

"You have so much to do for so many people," he said. I understood that I needed to go back and that the angels were pleading their case for me to do so, but I had a choice. I could go against this, if I wished.

The angel on my left said, "It's up to you. Do you want to stay or do you want to go?" The angels told me to look down. I saw my body on the ground with paramedics above it. Katrina stood to one side, looking at her phone. My vision of this was like a camera that zoomed in instantly. My angels and I were watching what unfolded in the scene together. I wondered...how am I here and there at the same time? I had heard of people seeing their body from above sometimes, but I was amazed with the realization that this stuff actually happens.

"Look again, so you'll know that this happened," the angel on my right side said.

"Yeah, you need the truth," said the one on my left.

At this point I remembered my conversation with God and how I needed to go back and tell everyone that God loved them. I knew, for the first time, that my angels were always there with me on earth. Telepathically, I asked them never to leave. They told me, without words, that they wouldn't. I looked down and told them I was going to go back. The angels acknowledged this. Immediately, my time out of my body was over.

I woke up in an ambulance, bewildered. I instantly blacked out. The next time I woke up I was in the hospital. The doctors told me I had been in a coma for three days. They called me a miracle as soon as I woke up. Katrina came to visit. She told me that I said a few words while lying on the ground. I said, "It burns," and "Help me," in a quiet voice. This must have been before leaving my body while I felt my skin burning from scrapes and cuts. The rest of the time on the ground I was unresponsive.

I don't remember much about my hospital stay. Physically, I was all messed up. My face was covered in contusions and bruises. I had road rash on my arms and legs. There were X-rays and many tests. I lay in a tunnel-like machine that scanned my brain and looked for other injuries. Smiling nurses entered my room asking, "How is the miracle doing today?" I first tried to eat some Jello but couldn't hold it down. I couldn't taste any of the food I put in my mouth. My balance was poor and I couldn't talk much either. My tongue got stuck when I tried to pronounce a word.

After a few days spent mostly sleeping and watching TV, I was discharged. I was pushed in a wheelchair out to Katrina's car. One of the nurses handed me a teddy bear called "Miracle."

As soon as I saw the concrete sidewalks outside of the hospital, I remembered that "boom" from when I first hit the ground. I looked up at the sky. I saw how bright white the sun was. The memory of my near death experience came flooding back. Things were different now. I felt my spirit had been freed.

Chapter 17

Discoveries

I ended up staying at Katrina's house for a few weeks while I recovered. It was comfortable and her kitchen was well stocked. I had the place to myself when she was at work and her kids were in school. I did my own physical therapy by working every day on my balance and speech.

Two days after I got back, I had an extremely vivid dream at around 3 or 4 AM. In this dream, I saw a field of grass and dirt where the first airplanes were being tested. It felt like time had been dislocated and I was literally there. I saw a vision of people testing the earliest versions of airplanes. The planes would roll forward on the grass, make it a few feet off the ground, then bounce back to earth. I knew they hadn't yet designed the wings with enough lift for the planes to stay up. In the dream, I heard a distant sound of trains, older sounding trains thundering on their tracks. It was scary. Why was God showing me this? I woke up with a scream and Katrina heard me. She turned on the light in the hall and stared at me questioningly.

"What happened?" she asked. We went to the kitchen and she gave me a glass of milk.

"I just had this bizarre dream that felt so real," I said. I told her about the planes. She nodded and agreed it was weird.

"I need to tell you something else too," I said. "When I jumped out of the car, I had this incredible experience. I met my guardian angels. There's more too."

"You did? Don't get mad at me but I'm not going to believe that. I don't believe in anything like that. But you can go ahead and tell me what happened."

"Okay. I'm going to break it down for you." I told her all the details of my near death experience. When it was over, she raised her eyebrows a little.

"Wow, that's crazy," she said. "Maybe it was another weird nightmare from hitting your head."

I knew it wasn't that. Immediately, I felt that I shouldn't have told her. She had always said that God, if there was a God to begin with, didn't care about us and that there wasn't anything after death.

"Something strange happened to me while you were in the hospital, though," Katrina went on to say. "After I followed you to the hospital, I realized I had no cash on me and I needed to get gas to drive home. I met someone in the waiting room who gave me change. This woman came out of nowhere and said she worked there. She told me her name but I forgot it. She said she knew who I was, although I didn't recognize her at all. She gave me lots of change that ended up being like $5 or $6, enough for me to get what I needed. When I went back to the hospital again, I went looking for her and eventually saw who I thought was the same person, but this time, she said she didn't work there. She didn't even seem to remember me. It was so odd."

I wasn't sure what to make of this incident. Maybe it was a miracle of a different kind. However, I was disappointed that Katrina didn't care about my amazing experience or want to understand more about what happened to me. I swore to myself that there *had* to be someone out there who knew what this was like.

In the coming weeks, with my head hurting with pounding migraines and my entire body aching, the world seemed different. And despite the pain, every time I looked up into the sky, especially a clear blue sky, I felt a sense of peace. I felt like I was still on the other side, feeling the love of God and my angels. There was a very warm sense of love and well-being deep in my heart.

I went on the internet. I had always been skeptical and questioned what I was taught in church years ago, but now I knew for sure my intuition did not lie. I went on my laptop and searched for every single religion. I studied various rules and beliefs and compared them to my experience. Along the way I started reading about things like the missing books of the Bible. There was so much information out there and so many opinions. I wasn't much of a reader and felt I wasn't going to find my answers in books. Considering what I had seen and felt with God, nothing seemed to match what I experienced. I felt very alone.

Next I watched shows on the internet and YouTube. I Googled with searches like "the truth behind God" and "what happens when you die." I came across something called a "Near Death Experience" or NDE. I started looking at videos and saw people who went through the same things I had. Some saw angels, guides, and loved ones. Some heard from God. It freaked me out at first, but only at first. Things were starting to make more sense.

Listening to ministers or deacons preaching in the church, or my relatives telling me I was going to hell, I felt that my mind and heart were in jail. I wondered why God couldn't Love me for who I was, for the very core of me. Now I knew I was Loved as an absolute Fact. There was no doubt and no need to look outside of myself to confirm it.

With my new knowledge, I realized I always had spiritual connections. I had just overlooked them and forgotten them. One day when I was four, my grandma had been sick. I came into the room and pointed at a picture of her mom and grandma. I told my grandma that they had visited me and told me she would get better and everything would be fine. Sure enough, the next day my grandma was well. My connection to the spiritual realm had been weakened during my years of trauma, addictions, and struggles just to get by. No wonder I had always been the weird, different one out of all my friends. Little did I know that there was still more to come.

One morning during my recovery, I was carefully getting out of the shower holding on to the stall and the sink. I had to concentrate on moving my feet deliberately because my sense of balance was still a little off. I definitely did not want to fall and hit my head again. Suddenly, I felt a rush of strong, familiar energy from my NDE. Voices came to me telepathically.

"We are your guardian angels. Empty your mind of everything you've ever known. We are going to teach you what you need to know."

Chapter 18

Pay Attention!

Many people with NDEs continue communicating with the other side. It happens differently for each person. Some call them entities but I just use the word angels. Whether I call them my guides, angels, or guardian angels, they have stayed with me just as they promised.

Sometimes I see a symbol of two angels my mind, but that's all I see visually. If they were to appear as they did in my NDE, I would be freaked out and they know that. Instead, we communicate telepathically. Many people wonder how telepathic communication works. What makes angel communication different from a typical thought is that you feel their emotions in your heart while you understand their thoughts in your head. Boom! You have the thoughts and messages of your guides.

Sometimes both guardian angels speak to me together. Sometimes one lets the other talk and waits his turn to speak. It's just like listening to people talking. I feel their personalities too. I know with my intuition coming through my heart who says what and how they say it. The angels speak clearly so I won't be confused. I don't know their names and don't need to. I don't think names even work the same way for them as they do for us.

My angels helped me heal from my injuries. Their voices came to me in the exact moments when I needed them. They were very much in tune with me every step of the way. They used to tell me how to walk, how to move, how to sleep. Information would come through in little tips. I would hear them and feel them saying "Put your back straight" or "Bend your knees a little." I could be lying in bed feeling uncomfortable, and they would say to turn my back a certain way. I learned there were many fine points to be aware of when it came to the positioning of the body.

The biggest lesson they taught me is how your mind controls everything. It all starts in your mind. Your thoughts turn into words and your words turn into actions. So watch your thoughts and words. The words you say create either positive or negative vibes. Think of every word that comes out of your mouth as a living being. When you say "I can't do it," that creates a negative outcome. When you say "I can do this!" or "Let's be positive!" or "Let's love each other and have unity," this helps a positive outcome more than you know. Your mind controls how you talk, how you walk, and how you feel. Your mind sends signals to your body and your body receives and sends signals to and from the minds of others. You basically can be anywhere in your mind, as weird as this sounds.

One day I was walking to the local grocery store with my headphones on. It's good meditation for me. It was a very bright and sunny day with a clear sky. Out of the blue, my angels said, "Breathe out of your heart area."

"What's that?" I asked in my mind.

"It's one of your energy fields. You have a lot of energy and light coming out of there."

"Oh, that's amazing."

"Yeah, so breathe from there."

I focused my breathing differently, just subtly. I felt a bit stronger.

"Do you know you have invisible wings?"

Of course, I did not know that.

"If you have trouble breathing, focus on breathing from your heart while focusing on your back." I have had shortness of breath all my life. Of course, the angels knew. That little technique they taught me made a difference.

"Focus your energies on your head," they said next.

"On the middle of my head?"

"On the sides or the temples. Wherever you feel yourself thinking. Use these energies to connect with people. This is your connection field. The most important one ever. You are going to use it every day, all the time."

The next few days I was focusing on these constantly. I noticed how I could feel people's emotions and their energies if I made the connection from specific areas in the energy field around my head. I noticed the little details of people's body language like I never had before. It was crazy to me to discover new layers in this reality filled with information I never picked up on before.

Next, my guides added something new. "Focus your energy on your spine," they said. "Straighten up your back. This is your spine and your spinal area is very powerful."

I agreed and I felt how powerful it was and how different I felt when I focused on my posture. This made me happy. I noticed how I started walking with more confidence, from the inside out, starting with focusing my mind on my spine. This mental focus flowed into how I appeared to people when I walked.

Then my angels asked me to focus on my knees. When I had social anxiety, my knees would get weak around people. This weakness changed and slowed my walking pace. I've learned that my angels love confidence, the kind that comes from loving ourselves and loving others with an open heart.

"Focus your energies on the backs of your knees. This is going to help your confidence when you walk," they said.

Thus far, I only knew about the energy fields in a few areas. I later went onto YouTube and searched for energy fields. I started reading about chakras. When I was scrolling through my search results, my guides told me to watch a specific video. "Pick that one," they said. This video explained the seven chakra fields. Chakras are specific important energy centers, but each part of the body is an energy field of its own. My angels have a way of breaking down the fine points of the human body and its connection to our minds.

Besides changing my own walk and posture, I started to pay attention to body language in other people. I saw how certain people were nervous when they walked and others were very self-assured.

To this day, my angels are always the ones telling me: pay attention, pay attention...PAY ATTENTION! They make me aware of human nature by pointing out the energy of people in different situations. When I'm around a bunch of people they'll say, "Pay attention to this woman. Look at how she is looking at her husband. Look how she is drifting away. She wishes she was happy. She wishes she had a good man." We have amazing conversations and I see the world and life in ways I never had before.

During the writing of this book, I passed a high school girl wearing an LA Dodgers jersey and tight black jeans. She was young, maybe in her freshman year. She carried a huge bookbag on her tiny shoulder. As she passed me, I smelled a huge waft of perfume. She was talking on her phone, telling someone in a sarcastic voice, "You could have come to get drunk with us but you didn't, and it's OK." I could tell she was very upset.

My angels telepathically communicated the emotion of sadness and pointed out a few things to notice in this situation. "She's in trouble and has no one to love her," they said.

The girl turned the corner and went out of sight, but the brief encounter made me wonder who she was trying to impress with all that perfume while still so young? And why was she getting drunk? What was going on at home that she was walking by herself with so much stuff in her bag? It couldn't all have been for school. Did she even have a home to begin with?

I had known many people like this growing up. They were desperately hoping that the hard mask of ego could hide their need for love. In my city, there are lots of people like this and it's normal for family to not be there for them. This high school girl could be in a situation like mine years ago. A lot of people act tough and grown up to cover up their pain. They are afraid to let their hearts show. I see more and more of this now.

I am aware how the insights I receive on people's minds could be used for evil. I realize how people warm up to you when you make them feel good inside. When you make people feel good, they want to be around you and tell you more because they trust you. This is how manipulative and narcissistic individuals can get into people's minds and fool them completely. This is why it's important to learn about energies and how our minds work, starting with yourself.

Some people might call connecting to the other side "meditation" or "prayer." I call it "kickin' it with my angels." It's just a matter of connecting to them however it happens. For instance, I may have my headphones on with any music I choose. I prefer my type of music but my angels will telepathically suggest a song I know they like. I put it on. That's a way I can spend time with them. Our music tastes overlap. I might be vibing to my music and they'll tell me, "That song's alright," but when I put on a song they like, I can feel them jamming. They get happy. They get excited. My angels like soulful music, music about love. The songs they don't like as much are materialistic songs, the songs only about money.

I can feel my angels when they party and when they dance. When I spread love and when I get love from other people, they get the most excited.

After I started listening to my angels, I never felt alone again. My angels helped make me who I am today. I didn't have much of a vocabulary before. They've taught me more clarity, more words, and better pronunciation. They just made me better all around. I am more concerned about my health than I was before. I've started taking care of myself. Even though I still love burgers, fries, and candy, I like eating healthier foods too, including greens.

I make sure they are involved in most decisions in my daily life. They teach me so many things and give me advice in particular moments. Even if I am deciding between one outfit and another, they help me coordinate just right. Whenever I do something big at work, create a video for YouTube, or even write a chapter for this book, they'll tell me they're so proud of me. They never put me down. And as for cursing, they don't like it, but they don't overreact if I slip up. I try to look out for them the best I can. Let's say I'm kicking it with my angels with the music on and say, "Oh shit, you guys remember when? Oh...My bad ya'll." They just laugh at me. Sometimes I catch myself from saying a curse word and they know it and tell me, "Go ahead and just say it. You're not going to be complete."

I got tired of retaining all the information that the angels teach me in my head so I started making YouTube videos. I don't sit down and plan what to say. I just let them talk for me, so to speak. To this day I love our relationship. It's like having someone always on your side who knows even the little things that go on in your life. I can be walking down the street and they'll remind me of something that happened recently. "Remember when you made that ham sandwich and dropped it on the floor? Yeah, that was funny," they start laughing, amused by how goofy life on earth can be. "We're just hazing you for being a rookie."

When they say things like this, I have to try so hard not to laugh in public because people would think I'm crazy.

The angels drew my attention to and helped me appreciate the clouds, the sky, and nature. One time I was walking in the rain to work because I didn't have a car. I was pissed. My angels asked me, "Would you rather not have any job at all? Or what if you were in a wheelchair and couldn't walk and you were still stuck in this rain without a car?"

I could only reply, "Dang, you guys are right." And when I happened to go to the local grocery store within the hour, there really was a guy in a wheelchair.

My angels said, "Look at that guy right there, you see him? He can't walk at all. What if you were like that? So just be grateful." My angels teach me to be grateful for absolutely everything. They remind me to be happy and notice the beauty all around me.

It's so cool learning about angels. However, my angels also taught me that they are limited. There was a time when I was so overwhelmed and excited to have my guardian angels to talk to that I forgot the Source. That's right—I wasn't talking to God at all! The angel on my right told me not to forget the importance of God. The one on the left reminded me about how much God loved me. The angels can help in the moment with decisions, but if I am asking for miracles in my life, I should not ask my angels but ask God directly. While angels can be involved with miracles such as urging me not to drive down a certain road where I'd have an accident, or giving me advice in challenging moments if I allow them to, the bigger miracles are for God alone. Angels can never overstep their boundaries.

The angels remind me of what I learned in my NDE—that God is not what many of us have been taught. People have to experience God for themselves in order to know the true nature of God's intelligence, light, and love. Long after my NDE, while feeling the love and happiness of my angels through telepathic communication, the angels reminded me they in turn get all their love and happiness from God. God is the Source and Creator of all. My angels reminded me that they too love God and that God loves me even more than they do. God is so powerful that these huge and powerful angels are a gift from him. I know from my NDE that this is the absolute truth.

Chapter 19

Discernment

Paying attention didn't just happen with random strangers on the street. With my old friends and in the city I grew up in, I started noticing details much more clearly. Sometimes my angels would point them out. Often I would just see them much faster than before.

One time a friend and I were going to the bus stop and I realized he was only hanging out with me because I had a pass to ride the bus for free. That's where what I call discernment came in. We started having a difficult discussion that ended with me calling him on it.

"You're only hanging out with me because of my pass," I said.

He got really upset. "I wouldn't hang out with you because of that! That's fucked up. Why are you being a hater?"

I could see that when someone gets upset like that, all defensive and throwing the blame, it means they are guilty.

After my NDE, there came a time when I wasn't doing so well financially. I lost work and my apartment and had to move back in with Aunt Sara. Her place was still messy, with horrible smells and piles of junk. She was getting older and starting to have health issues. At first, I was supposed to be there as my aunt's in-home care provider, but she changed her mind on wanting me to do it. She didn't want me to get paid because she wanted me to depend on her. And she didn't want me to borrow her car to go on job searches. Instead of arguing with her about it, which wouldn't have done any good, whenever I went to the grocery store, I stopped at the local library and updated my resume. I put in applications everywhere and started going to job interviews while doing other errands without telling her. This kept the peace in the house, although she still tried to mess with me.

"Pay attention to what she's doing in the kitchen," my angels said. Out of the corner of my eye I caught her in the refrigerator spitting on my soda and wiping the spit all over the lid. I threw that soda out. Other times, I saw her spit in a cup and stir it with liquor and take it to her friends and laugh. Obviously, I didn't want to bring any food into the kitchen. Instead of being angry at how she behaved, I started feeling bad for her. She had no idea what God's love is like. If you have God's love, you don't ever hurt anyone on purpose. I learned exactly how to keep my food safe and out of her reach. One time when she was out I lit some incense for its beautiful smell, focused on the light of the flame, and sent love to her.

During my NDE, I learned that God likes cleanliness in the sense that we treat ourselves and our surroundings with respect. When we love ourselves and others, we naturally want to be at our best. Aunt Sara, at the bottom of it, was vicious towards others because she was unhappy with herself. She didn't want to keep her place neat or throw anything out. In time, she became indifferent to paying bills to the point where all utilities got cut off. This was all a reflection of her troubles on the inside.

With my discernment, and knowing what I did about NDEs, I started to see how the effects of her actions were coming back at her, energetically. Many people who have had an NDE tell you that they had something called a life review. They saw and felt exactly what they had done to others from the recipients' point of view, whether to hurt them or help them. When you're experiencing this life review, you feel exactly what the other person felt. Sometimes the results of our actions in life come back to us as we're living. I saw this with Aunt Sara.

During the time I lived with her, Aunt Sara started staying in bed for many hours during the daytime. My angels pointed out that she stayed in her room crying a lot when no one was around. But whenever I arrived, boom! She came out of her room and announced, "Oh, let me start my day now." When I left, she said, "I guess I am going to sleep now." I sensed that she was very depressed.

One day while she was resting in bed, there was a quiet, peaceful moment. The TV was playing with the volume low but Aunt Sara wasn't even watching. I saw her head turned and she was looking out the window. The sun was setting and there was only dim light coming in. I muted the TV volume and sat at the side of her bed.

"Aunt Sara, there's something I want to tell you. I had an accident and hit my head two years ago. I left my body and met my guardian angels. It's called a near death experience or NDE."

"Oh. Okay, Chris. That's nice," she said, looking away. She was so down that I couldn't make her understand or even take interest in what I had to say. She was going through something deep inside. I had noticed that Aunt Sara's phone didn't ring much anymore, and she had no one to call. A lot of people had found out how Aunt Sara really was. Her lies had been exposed. Aunt Sara had lived her life interfering with and hurting other people but now she was alone to face harsh truths about how she had acted.

My discernment let me see that Aunt Sara realized she had done wrong to me and many others, but she wouldn't apologize. Her suffering was intense and constant. I felt horrible and sad to see it. Her guilt was wearing her down. Every time I went to her house after a few days without seeing her, she had no stamina. One time she could hardly close the door to her car because she was weak she could barely move. When I went to see her before work, her face brightened somewhat. This wasn't the case years before when we were constantly bickering.

After nine months of job searching, the local school district invited me to come test for a crossing guard position. I passed the test. In the school district conference room with a huge round table and dark leather chairs, I had paid training and orientation. At Aunt Sara's place, I hadn't felt like I was contributing to the world or to my future. I was so happy to finally have a job again. As soon as I could, I moved out and got my own place. Life was more peaceful when I was away from her. But I am not the kind of person who holds grudges. And I was the only one to visit her on a regular basis to see how she was doing. There was nothing I could do but be good to her and show her love.

My friendships started to shift as well. Discernment teaches you people's true intentions. You can see whether they are coming from a good or bad place inside. You know someone's spiritual inside—you see, you feel, you sense. You see what they really think about you as opposed to what they put out to your face.

Before my NDE, if a girl wanted to hang out with me for her own convenience I would drop everything. When my true self got awakened, I wasn't so eager to please. When she would say, "Let's hang out," I would counter with, "Why don't we hang out later instead?" I noticed very often that these girls immediately changed their minds saying, "Ohhh, we don't have to hang out after all. Good night." There were times when my angels would tell me, "Pay attention to her body language. Listen to her tone. Listen to how she says 'I love you'. She's lying to you. She was not with her mom last night like she said."

I also saw, so clearly, that when I worked on music and songs with certain people, they would get jealous when my verses were better. Many people let their egos get in the way instead of living with gratitude and curiosity. I stopped working in music because my equipment went out of commission. Certain friends became irritated because I was always positive. I was always making light of a situation because that's what we are supposed to do—bring light into the world. Unfortunately, when someone's miserable, they want you to be miserable too. I found myself surrounded by many miserable people. We seemed so far apart. My NDE taught me to be positive and it taught me love. I noticed how some people didn't like that I was happy. These were the sarcastic and cynical ones, always in a bad mood. I realized I was outgrowing them. When you outgrow people, there is nothing to talk about when you hang out. It becomes boring and drains your energy.

Events were showing me who my friends were and who they weren't. When I told Eric and Mike about my NDE, they were excited. "That's dope! I want to hear all about this! I've got to watch more videos about this stuff!" they said, eager to learn more. A few others supported me like this too. However, it was ironic that the one person who had who literally stood over my dead body while I met God and my angels, who had generously helped me recover in her own home, never believed me. Katrina mocked my experience, and didn't believe anything relating to my angels.

"It's ghosts. You talk to ghosts!" Katrina said.

"No, it's not ghosts," I said. "These are my guides. My angels are like real people to me, as real as you are. I feel them in my heart. It's the exact same feeling, the exact same voices, same everything as in my NDE, so I know they are real! Now I hear them but when I died I saw them too!"

Katrina gave a sarcastic laugh. "Come on. There's nothing like that out there. It's imaginary, all in your head. You're living in a fantasy world so you can avoid reality. The fact is that the world is fucked up. And then you die," she said.

I felt horrible that Katrina had no emotion or feeling for what happened to me. Her negative energy was like a slap to my face. But instead of feeling upset, I focused on understanding her and feeling compassion. She was a person who needed love, but was not awakened to love yet. She kept strong shields around her that prevented her from feeling or accepting love from others. She thought she could gain love by being a player, but that wasn't really love. I realized it was not healthy for me to be around her. We had to part ways.

My angels proved to be right about the mindset and intentions of many people, but I still saw the good in all of them. I became more accepting and understanding of others than ever before. Many people are confused and it's not their fault. Not everyone in life knows their purpose but that is fine. God still loves them. Everybody is here for a reason, and those reasons are huge. This is true for each and every one of us. It's humbling when you realize this.

One time, my angels gave me specific messages on humility. Being humble is being strong enough to accept imperfections in yourself and in others. The first key to humility is to appreciate what people do for you. Tell people how important they are to you. Tell them you love them. They just may need to hear it at the exact time that you are around. Don't hold back. Next, respect people's views, no matter what their backgrounds, races, or religions. Even if you disagree with an opinion, understand that there is always a reason why people act or think the way they do. No one is perfect. If we were perfect, we would be boring. The last key to being humble is forgiveness. Continue to do good to people even when they screw you over. The best way to kill hate is to love someone. Just because someone is a certain way does not mean you have to be the same way. You don't have to be bigger but you have to be smarter and wiser. Show love. Hate will come back to you if you show hate. Misery is the result. That is no way for anyone to live.

My angels told me that life is like a plane ride. When we are newborns, we are still on the ground. Once we start walking and talking, we are flying. It's going to be a long, long flight with lots of turbulence. Angels are the pilots to help us get through. They're going to give us hints and clues when our time is coming, whether it is time for an important change in our life or time to get ready for death, which is a new life. At the final destination, angels will be there to tell you to unbuckle your seatbelt, thank you for flying with them, and good luck in the afterlife.

Chapter 20

Life as an NDEr

Many people ask how my life is different after my NDE. I am happier and more at peace. Many things that bothered me before don't bother me now. In situations where I might get mad at someone in the past, I now see their reason for doing what they did. I am not afraid of dying or of hell anymore. I enjoy life instead of worrying about what others think of me. My experience taught me how to treat people, not through rules or guidelines, but simply based on the love I feel within. I feel more compassion for other people and so much more empathy. Although I never liked hurting anyone's feelings before, that feeling is now much stronger. I don't like telling a lie and can't tell one without feeling like a piece of shit afterwards.

My spiritual side is like a free-spirited hippie wearing rainbow colors and talking about peace, the type of person I didn't consider myself before. There are many people who have spiritual tendencies and don't even know it. A spiritual person doesn't judge you, no matter how you look. Spiritual people don't see appearances. We see spirits and we see the good in even the most damaged person. A spiritual person tries to get better every day. I am very open to learning about new opinions and ideas, especially spiritual ones. Anything that has you searching for God is what it's all about. Trying to help people is the main objective of life and becomes your mission. I want to motivate people who went through the same things that I did.

After my NDE, I can sense the spiritual realm all around us. I automatically pay attention to it. There are invisible spirits walking the earth. Some just come and go. For instance, an angel might briefly appear just to warn us to avoid an accident. There are no set rules.

And I sense the vibrations of people around me, even when I am out in public in a big crowd. I know when people are happy that I am doing well, or when they think that I shouldn't be drunk in public.

I now perceive nature differently too. Whenever I look at tree or a plant, I notice little aspects that I never saw before. I feel how alive plants are on many levels. I notice whenever plants are sick or dying. They are precious to me and I even talk to them. Animals seem different too. I notice how similar they are to humans. In the quiet pauses between the barks of dogs and meows of cats, I hear them communicating certain words and thoughts. And I pay attention to the purity of my drinking water. Whenever I go by a lake, I feel the presence of God very strongly. There are reminders of my NDE everywhere.

Since my NDE, I have been far too happy inside to go down the road of addictions again. My social anxiety has disappeared. I am not concerned with people looking at me because I sense people's souls and intuitively understand the situation. Instead of my mind racing into thoughts of someone making fun of me, I pay attention to the love in people. Instead of being paranoid of people judging my appearance, my mind focuses on how I will be genuinely liked when I treat people with love. My fear of public speaking is gone and I have shared my story on many NDE radio shows. I never rehearse what to say because I am confident that with help from the other side I will do just fine.

In my research into the spiritual world, I came across the International Association for Near Death Studies (IANDS). I went through Facebook and found many groups. I joined some and ran across new people who went through the same thing I had. I made a new circle of friends. They took me under their wing. What I noticed right away was that they were so nice to me and open hearted. They showed me the same kind of love I felt on the other side. I love my spiritual friends because I don't have to hide who I am when it comes to them.

I applied to the 2018 IANDS conference just before the deadline when I was sick with the flu. A few months later, I found out I was accepted. I was so happy. I didn't have enough money to cover the travel expenses, but I remembered George, Aunt Poochie's first husband, who had given me his number years ago and still kept in touch with the family. I called him, explained about my near death experience, and why I wanted to go to the conference. I asked if he could help me.

"You died? You're speaking in front of people? Damn, I'm proud. Say no more," George said. He helped book my flight to Seattle. This was only my second time on an airplane.

I got a ride to the airport from an amazing friend, Janet, who used to live in the same apartment building as Aunt Sara. I arrived in Seattle at 3 AM on the day I was supposed to speak. I caught a taxi from the airport to the hotel. Early in the morning, I was still wide awake and hungry so I walked to a Jack in the Box about 10 minutes from my hotel and got some food. As I walked back to the hotel, some guy honked at me.

"Hey bro!" he called out. I wasn't used to people being friendly like that at that time of day.

"Whoa! I'm from California. We don't do that stuff out there," I answered, laughing.

"We do that stuff out here! Welcome to Washington. Hey! I'm so drunk and I just got back from the club. I got all the good weed!"

"Thanks but you know what...I'm fine! I don't think I need it." I left out the part about speaking on an NDE panel in just a few hours. That would be just too hard to explain.

"I appreciate you, man. Have a good one." The light went green and he took off.

I got what sleep I could in my hotel room, woke up a few hours later, and took a shower. The presentations were downstairs in several large rooms. I was in time to hear a presentation by my friend Tricia Barker, a college professor from Texas who had an NDE during back surgery after a car accident. Angels helped in her healing too. It was amazing to hear her story in person.

Between the presentations, so many people mingled and gathered around me, welcoming me to the NDE community. They asked me when I was going to speak. I was scheduled for two hours later. I was wearing my green dress shirt and black pants with new blue shoes I had bought just the day before. I tried to distract myself from the thought of speaking in front of people I never met before and decided to call George.

"I'm nervous!" I told him.

He laughed. "My brother, I have a feeling you are going to make them love you! You are already ahead of the game."

"Why?"

"You come from a bad city and I know you are embarrassed that they will judge you out there but guess what, my friend? If you want to hide your NDE from them,

94

put it in a book, because many people don't read. Get out there and give that audience the truth."

"Damn, man. You're right. I'm going to kill this, George!" We both laughed because that wasn't the best word to use when describing a near death experience.

After meditating with my headphones for a while, I spoke on an NDE panel with two other survivors of childhood abuse. I began with the words, "So, my name is Chris. I'm an NDEr," and something just took over. It must have been my angels helping me. Even the suicide attempt came out as a funny, positive thing. It was the story of how I tried to kill myself, only to learn to love myself and be happy. My NDE really was the best thing that ever happened to me.

When I finished, my angels, the ones on my right and my left, tapped me on the back and told me I did it! I briefly called George who told me he was so proud of everything I was doing. In the hours to come, lines of people caught my attention, telling me how they enjoyed hearing me speak. I was tugged by my sleeves in many directions! This felt like a family reunion with people who loved you for who you were inside. I finally had the family that I always wanted, people who could truly relate to me and understand me.

As I flew home, I felt refreshed. I returned as a more positive and enlightened soul.

Chapter 21

Forgiveness

I was working one day in the rain at my crossing guard job, helping kids and parents cross the intersection. It was hectic after school and I had been outside for a long time, bundled up against the cold. Finally I got a chance to check my phone and there was a voicemail from Aunt Sara.

"Your grandma is in the hospital," she said. "Can you come over after work so we can go see her?"

It was still raining hard when I drove over to Aunt Sara's place and picked her up to go to the hospital. I held the umbrella over Aunt Sara as she got out of the car in the hospital parking lot. At the desk, we asked for directions to my grandma's room and went down several halls to find it.

Aunt Sara glanced at my grandma as she lay in the hospital bed and sat down on a chair. "You look good," she said. "You'll be home in a few days." Aunt Sara crossed her arms and sat there as rain poured against the windows.

I didn't agree with what Aunt Sara said. I didn't think my grandma looked like herself at all. I saw pain and fear in her face. I knew she wasn't going to make it. My angels were making me feel her energy. They showed me all that she was thinking. She was revisiting her life in her mind. It was the deepest emotional and spiritual connection I had ever experienced with my angels. My angels said she was going to be with them so not to worry.

"Ask whether she is eating," my angels said. I went over and held my grandma's hand. When the nurse came in, I asked about her appetite. The nurse said she was throwing up everything she ate.

"That's no good, Grandma!" I said. "We can't have anything like that going on!" I smiled at her. She laughed but when she looked at my face she got sad again.

With my encouragement, my grandma ate a couple of pieces of chicken. I asked her to drink some orange juice for me. She did. My grandma looked into my eyes and broke down crying. She was so dehydrated that she had no tears.

"I want to get out of here," she told me. I felt exactly what she meant when she said get out of there. She wanted to get out of this situation on earth where she felt sick and suffered. But she was trying to make peace before she left. I felt so much sincerity from her. She was so scared, she was so sad, and she was so ashamed of how she had treated me years ago. Many times she had beaten me and called me bad names. She used to tell me that she wished I had been aborted, just like my mom told me. Grandma remembered it all in the hospital and felt such pain over it.

I looked at her and told her without words that it was okay; I forgave her for everything she'd ever done. I spoke just four words, "I got you, Grandma!"

A couple days later I was on a lunch break from my crossing guard job when I got the call that Grandma was passing on. At the wake, she looked very peaceful in her casket. I knew she was finally at rest in body and soul.

I saw Aunt Poochie and Aunt Laura at the funeral. They looked a little surprised to see me. Both asked me how I was, but I could tell neither wanted to talk much. I said I was fine. I took my seat in the church. I looked around for my mom, but she never showed.

After the funeral, I ended up forgiving all my family members in my heart. This went for everybody including my parents. I haven't seen my mom since my NDE, so she probably has no idea about all the changes in my life since then.

After six months as a crossing guard, I felt I could do more in my career. I applied for a job with special education kids. My application was accepted and I started to work in the classroom as a para educator, a "para" for short. I became part of the regular school staff. As a para, there are many things you do to help kids, from teaching math to changing their diapers. Some kids are in wheelchairs and others you need to guide from the bus stop by holding their hands. Some are verbal and some are nonverbal. There are kids who run from you or who bite, kick, or spit on you. A lot of these kids are different, but as a para, you know what you signed up for.

After six months as a para educator, I tested to become a para translator, which is similar but focuses on deaf and hard of hearing kids. A month later, I got the results. I was told I passed the test with high scores. I had taken courses in American Sign Language before my NDE simply because I liked signing; now I finally get to use what I learned.

As a para educator, I am the substitute if the teacher doesn't come in. As a para translator, I do signing for deaf and hard of hearing kids. I love what I do. It feels natural to me since I grew up with ADHD. I was different myself. When I stand in the classroom with kids learning math and social studies, I get deep into the lectures too. I get animated about whatever they're learning. There's a lot of stuff I have forgotten, especially about history! The good thing is, when I'm excited about the lectures, so are the kids. They pay attention when Mr. Chris is there!

My work is very spiritual too. On the surface, it's hard to tell how some special education kids are feeling because their senses of vision, sight, hearing, taste, and touch are different. I use my discernment all the time. I've worked long enough to tell when a child is crying for real or faking it. Occasionally, my angels will pop in with messages like, "Let him touch the boards," because some kids are tactile and learn through touching things. My angels can also pinpoint the subtle reasons why a kid won't listen to one para but will listen to another.

I love how special needs kids are very in touch with the spiritual world. I notice the details of how the kids interact with each other, especially when they are very young or don't talk. They have their own non-verbal lingo. They might just sit there and look at each other, but if you pay attention, you can tell that they're feeling each other's emotions. One might smile and the other one smiles back. One might look serious and another one notices and looks serious too. If someone is crying, another comes up and quietly puts an arm around them.

When I work with Down syndrome kids, I notice how they are more honest than most "normal" people. They always look at each other when talking and are very straightforward about their feelings. One will tell another, "I don't like when you get that close to me," and the response will simply be, "Oh, sorry. Bye." But they eventually make up with a hug and don't hold any grudges.

Kids with intellectual disabilities like this aren't ashamed or embarrassed about themselves. They don't doubt that they can learn karate or get a job and a place, or get married someday. So when you see a kid in a wheelchair who can't speak and is wearing a helmet, don't think that kid is below you. Sometimes what we lack in the physical we get in the mental or spiritual. People who look like they have it all in the physical world can be lacking spiritually. It is very important to balance these things.

My angels have been with me every step of the way. In addition to working with kids, another mission of my life is to be involved with the angel realm and to communicate about them. Working with angels is all about energy— connecting with energy from a pure heart and healing the world with it. I feel peoples' energy right off the top, and I feel it deep too.

I still go by the neighborhood I grew up in, but I don't feel bad or alone there anymore. Now I just reflect on life and see the love there. When I run into someone who recognizes me from years ago, we always have a great conversation.

Now and then strangers see me talking to my angels and call out, "Who the fuck are you talking to?" I just wave to them and smile; it's too hard to explain. My main message to them, as to everyone, is what I learned from my near death experience. No matter who they are or what they do, God will go to the ends of the earth to show them that they are loved.

Printed in Great Britain
by Amazon

68134125R00069